Joseph
HAYDN

CELLO CONCERTO
IN D MAJOR

Hob. VIIb:2

Edited by
Clark McAlister

Study Score
Partitur

SERENISSIMA MUSIC, INC.

ORCHESTRA

2 Oboes

2 Horns (D)

Violins I

Violins II

Violas

Violoncellos

Double Basses

Duration: ca. 25 minutes

Premiere: 1783 or 1784 (conjecture)
Probably in Esterházy Castle
Antonín Kraft, cello solo
Esterházy Court Orchestra / Composer

This study score is an unabridged licensed reprint – in reduced format – of the large conductor's score
first issued by Kalmus. The large score and a complete set of parts are available for sale from the Kalmus
catalog as number A 1577.

Edwin F. Kalmus, LC
P. O. Box 5011
Boca Raton, FL 33431-0811
Phone: 561-241-6340; 800-434-6340
Fax: 561-241-6347
Website: www.efkalmus.com

ISMN: 979-0-58042-132-6
This score is a newly engraved urtext edition prepared
from the composer's holograph and other primary sources.

Printed in the USA
First Printing: September, 2018

CELLO CONCERTO
Hob.VIIb:2 (Op.101)

JOSEPH HAYDN
Practical Performing Edition by Clark McAlister

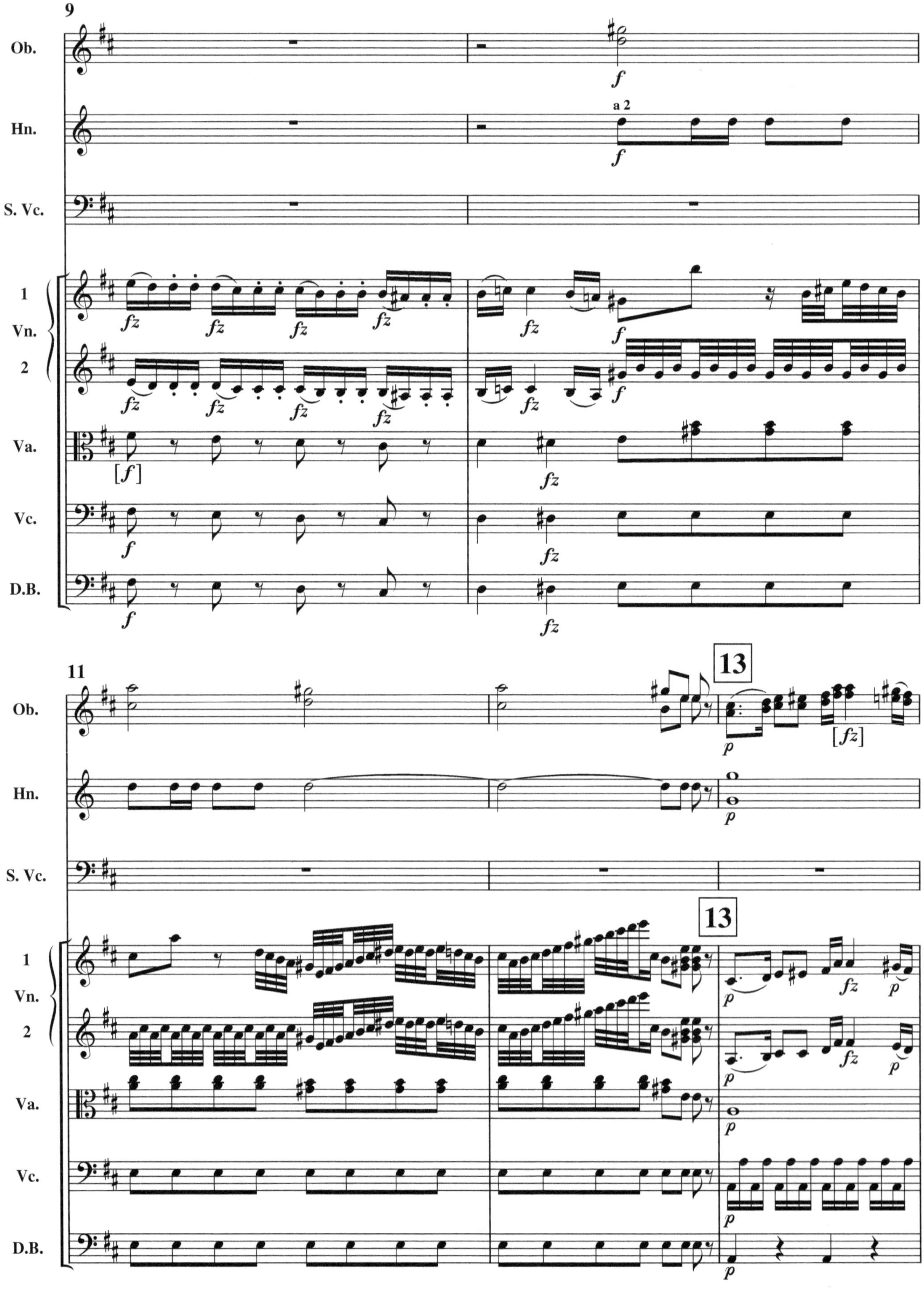
9
Ob.
Hn.
a 2
S. Vc.
1
Vn.
2
Va.
[f]
Vc.
D.B.
11
13
[fz]

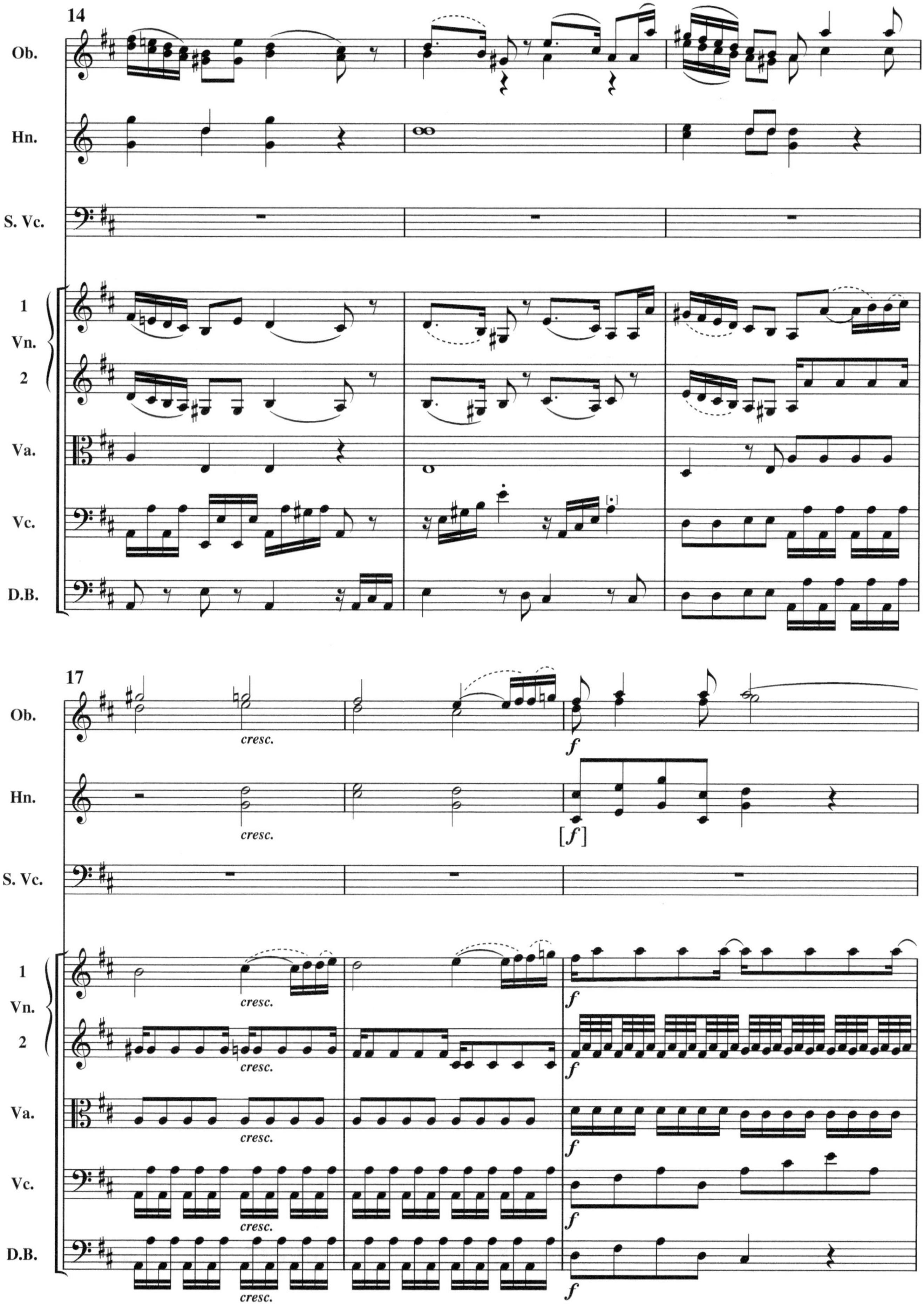
14
Ob.
Hn.
S. Vc.
1
Vn.
2
Va.
Vc.
D.B.
17
cresc.
f
[f]

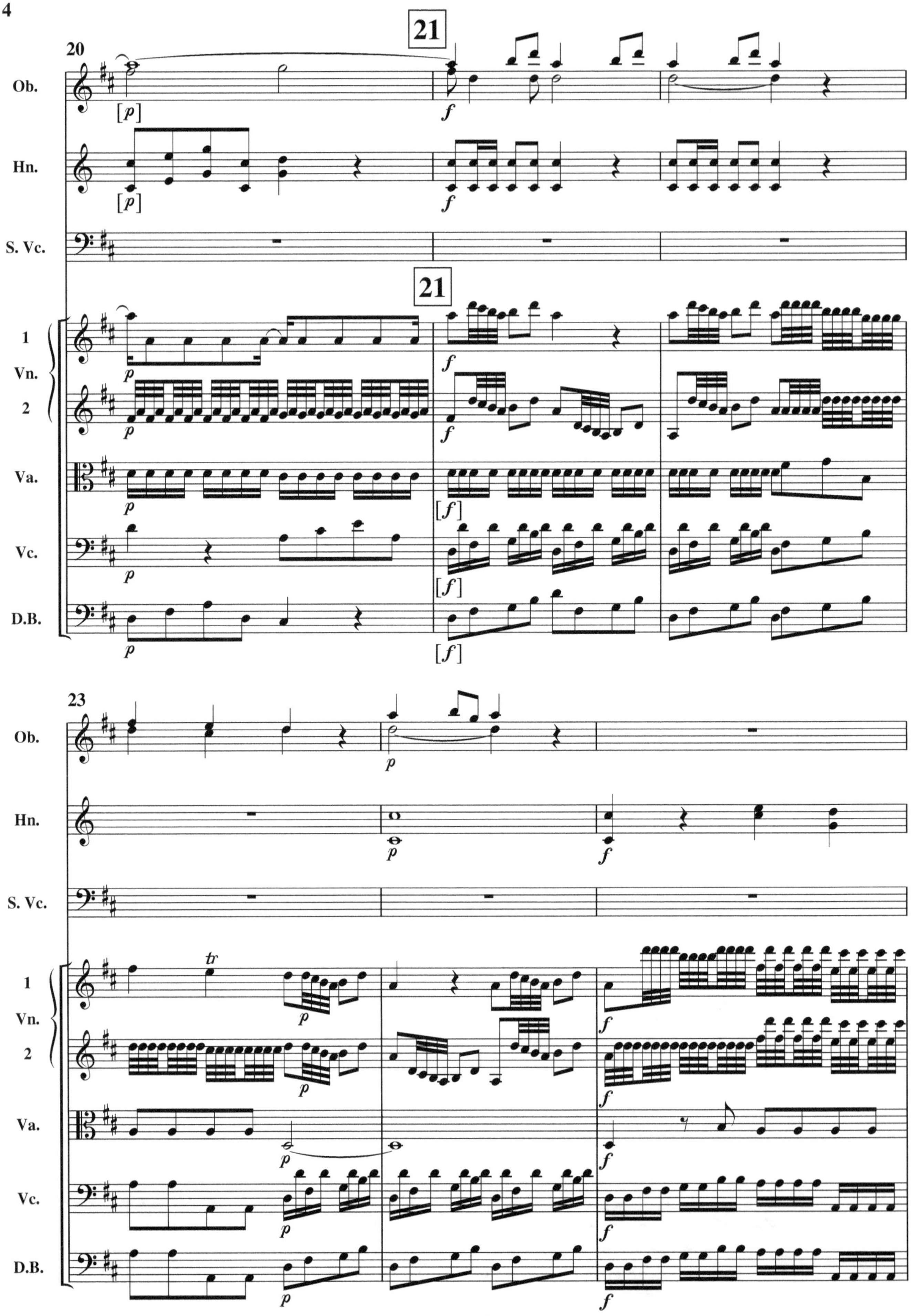
20
21
Ob.
Hn.
S. Vc.
1
Vn.
2
Va.
Vc.
D.B.
[p]
[f]
p
f
tr
23

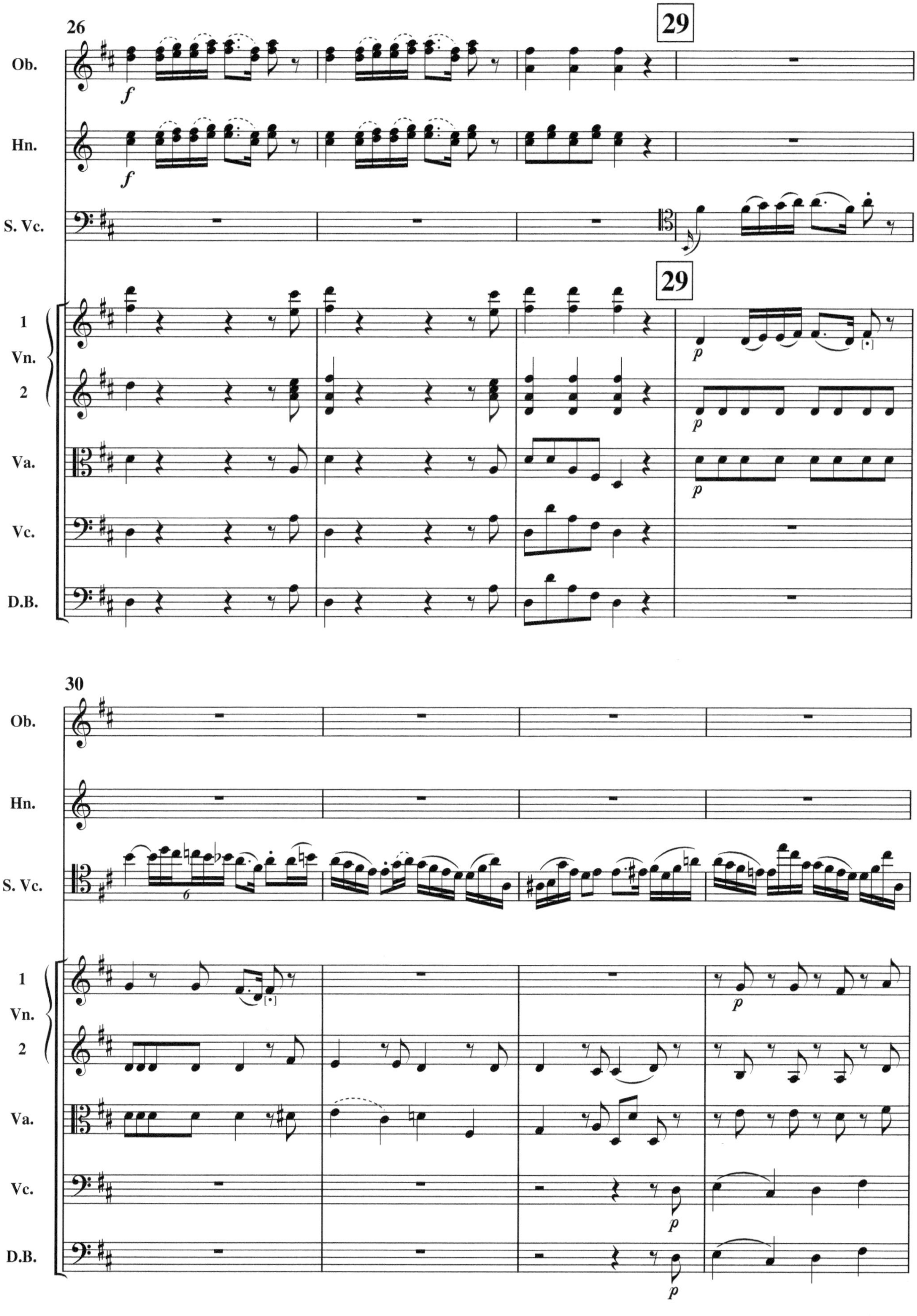
26
29
Ob.
Hn.
S. Vc.
1
Vn.
2
Va.
Vc.
D.B.
f
p
[•]
30
6

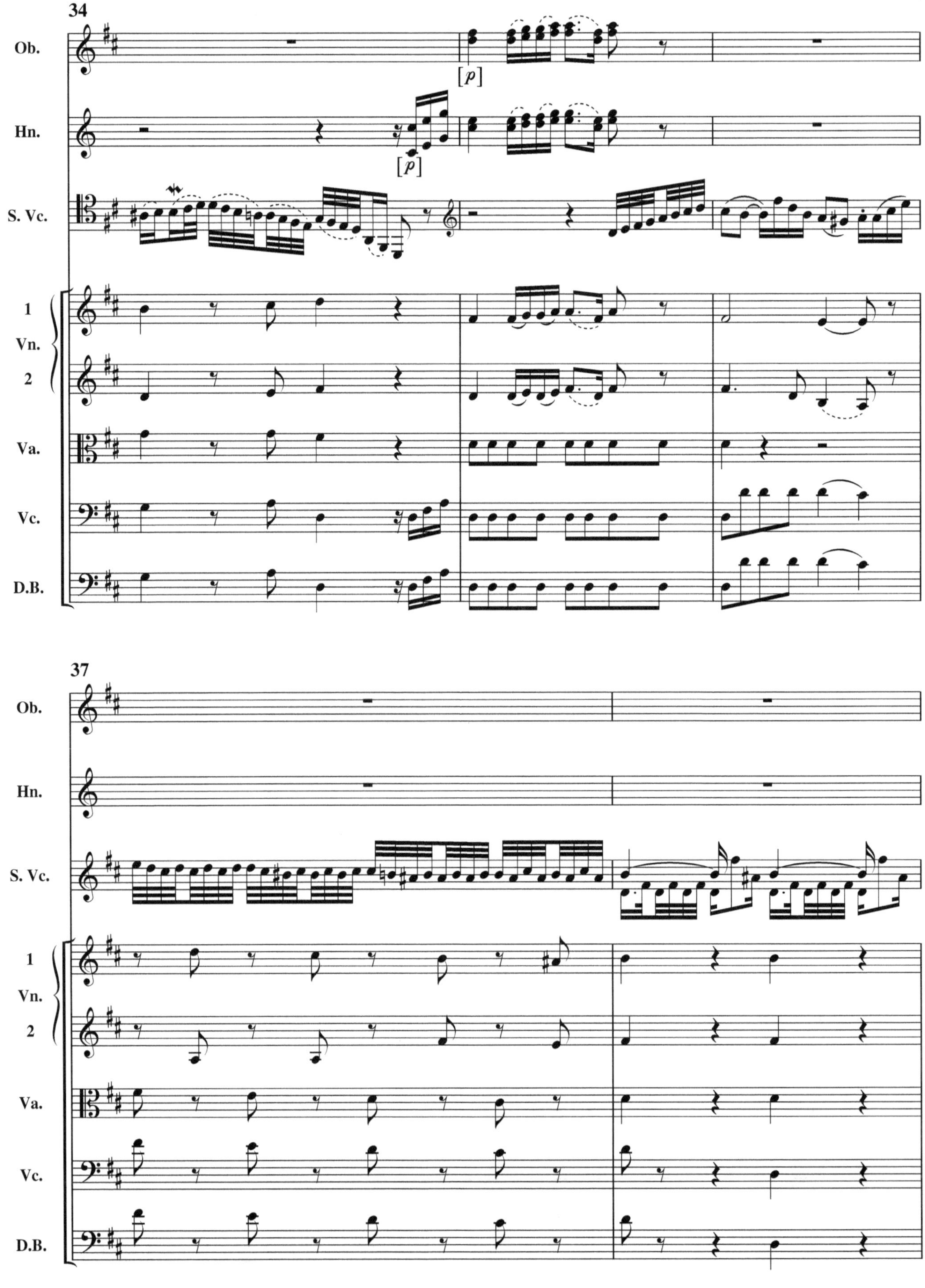
34
Ob.
[p]
Hn.
[p]
S. Vc.
1
Vn.
2
Va.
Vc.
D.B.
37
Ob.
Hn.
S. Vc.
1
Vn.
2
Va.
Vc.
D.B.

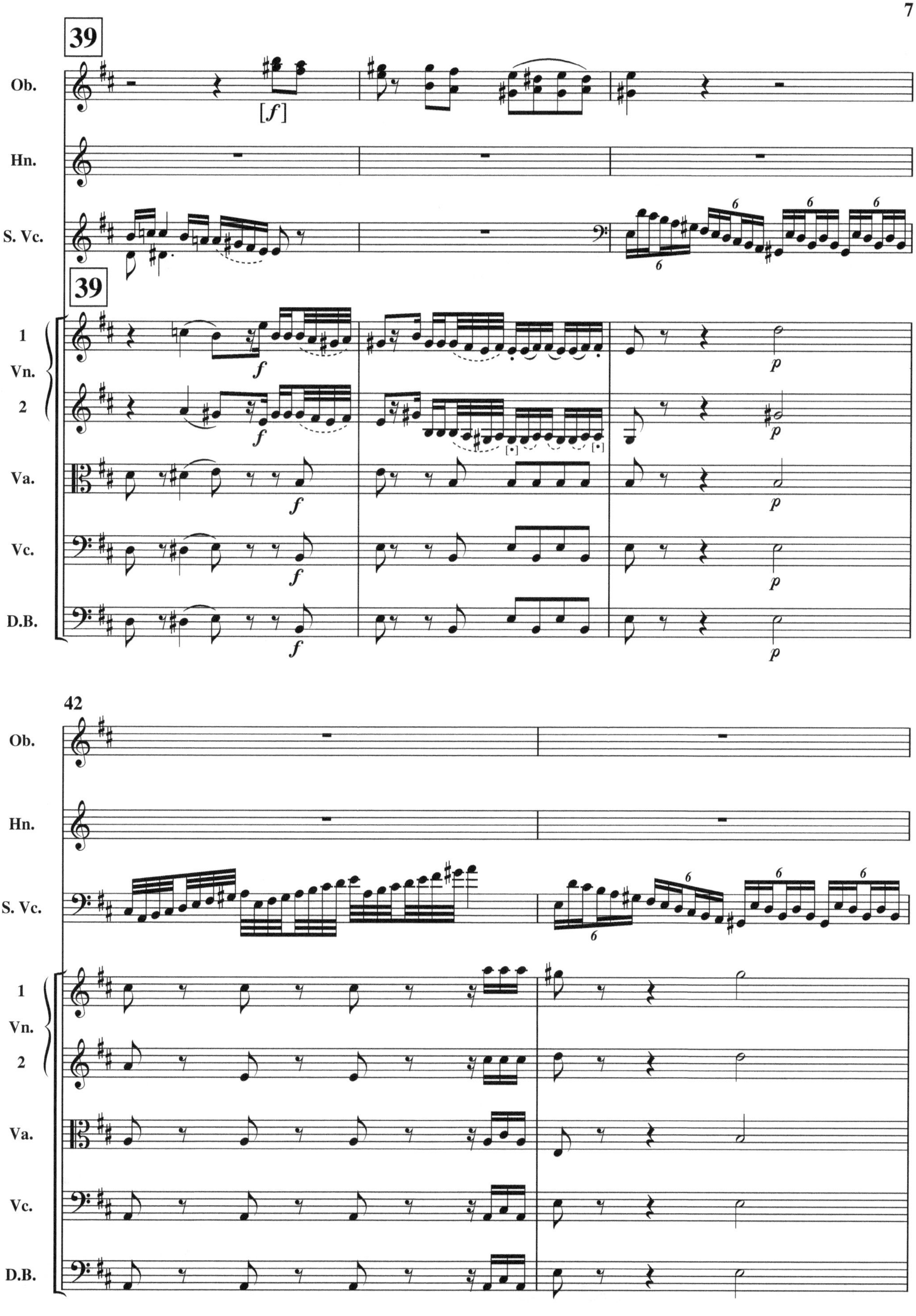
39
Ob.
Hn.
S. Vc.
Vn. 1 2
Va.
Vc.
D.B.
[f]
f
p
6
42

44
Ob.
Hn.
S. Vc.
6
6
1
Vn.
2
Va.
Vc.
D.B.
47
46
Ob.
[f]
Hn.
[f]
S. Vc.
tr
47
1
Vn.
2
[cresc.]
f
[cresc.]
f
Va.
[cresc.]
f
Vc.
[cresc.]
f
D.B.
[cresc.]
f

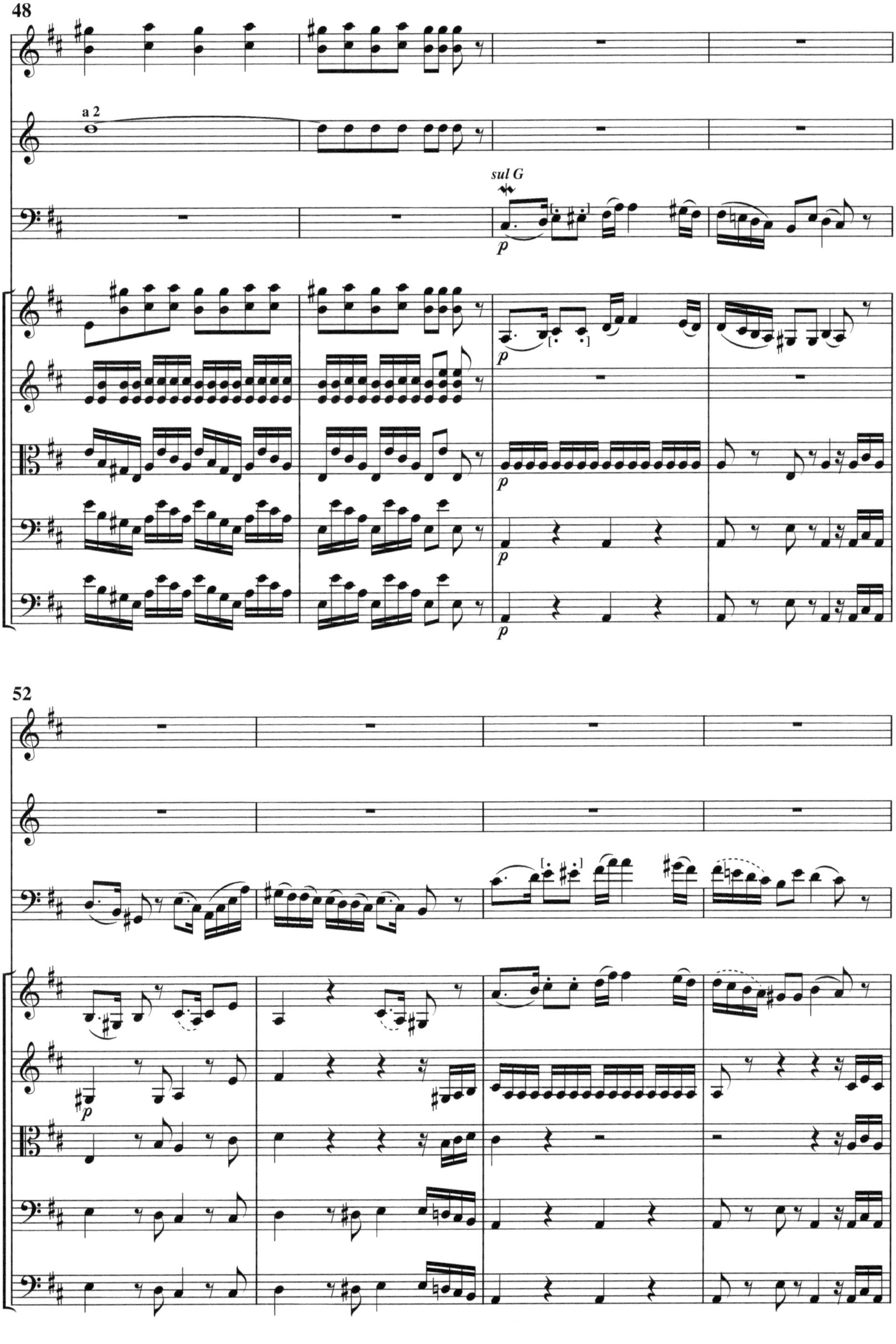
48
Ob.
Hn.
a 2
S. Vc.
sul G
p
1
Vn.
2
Va.
Vc.
D.B.
52

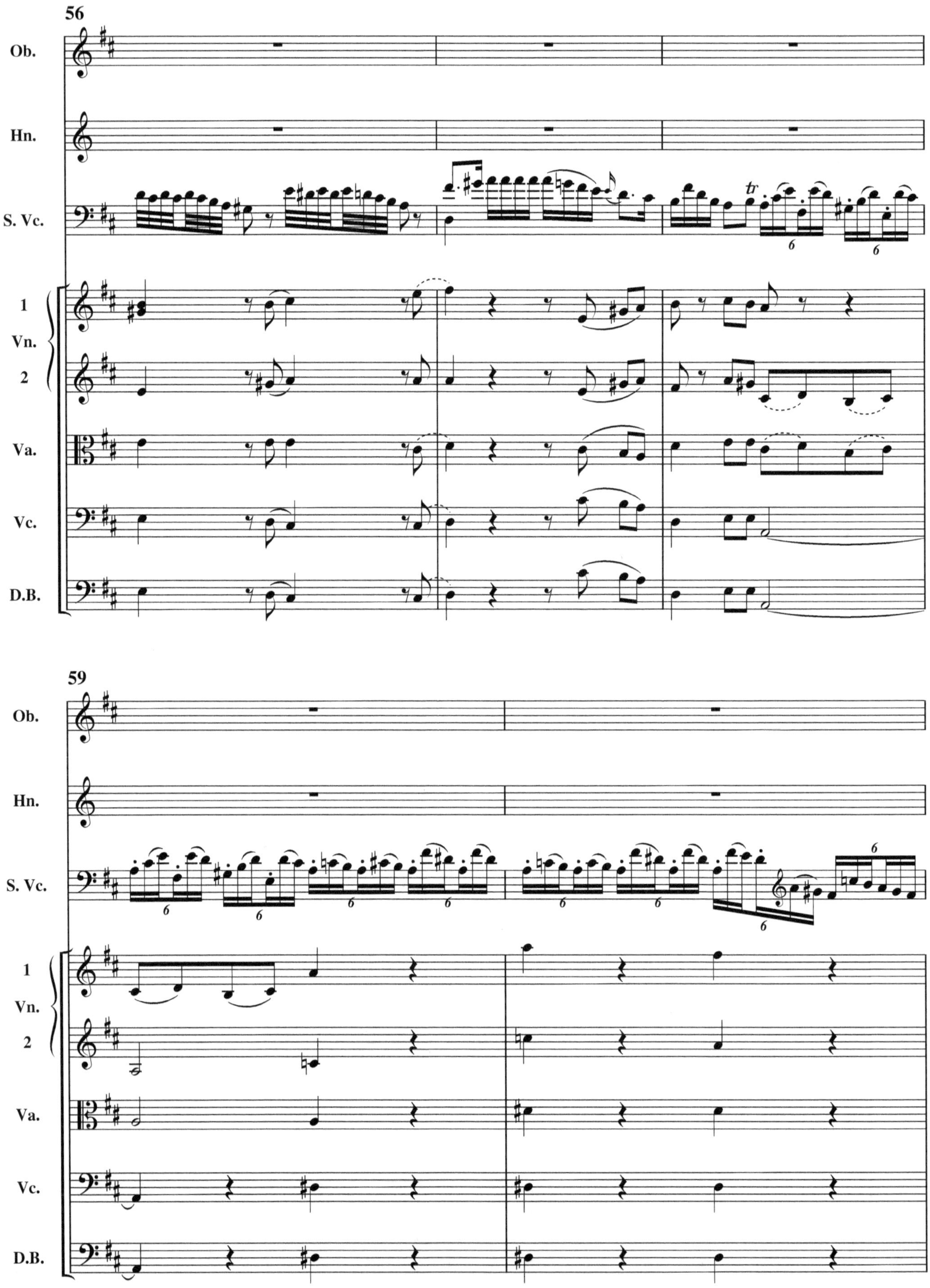
56
Ob.
Hn.
S. Vc.
1
Vn.
2
Va.
Vc.
D.B.
59
Ob.
Hn.
S. Vc.
1
Vn.
2
Va.
Vc.
D.B.

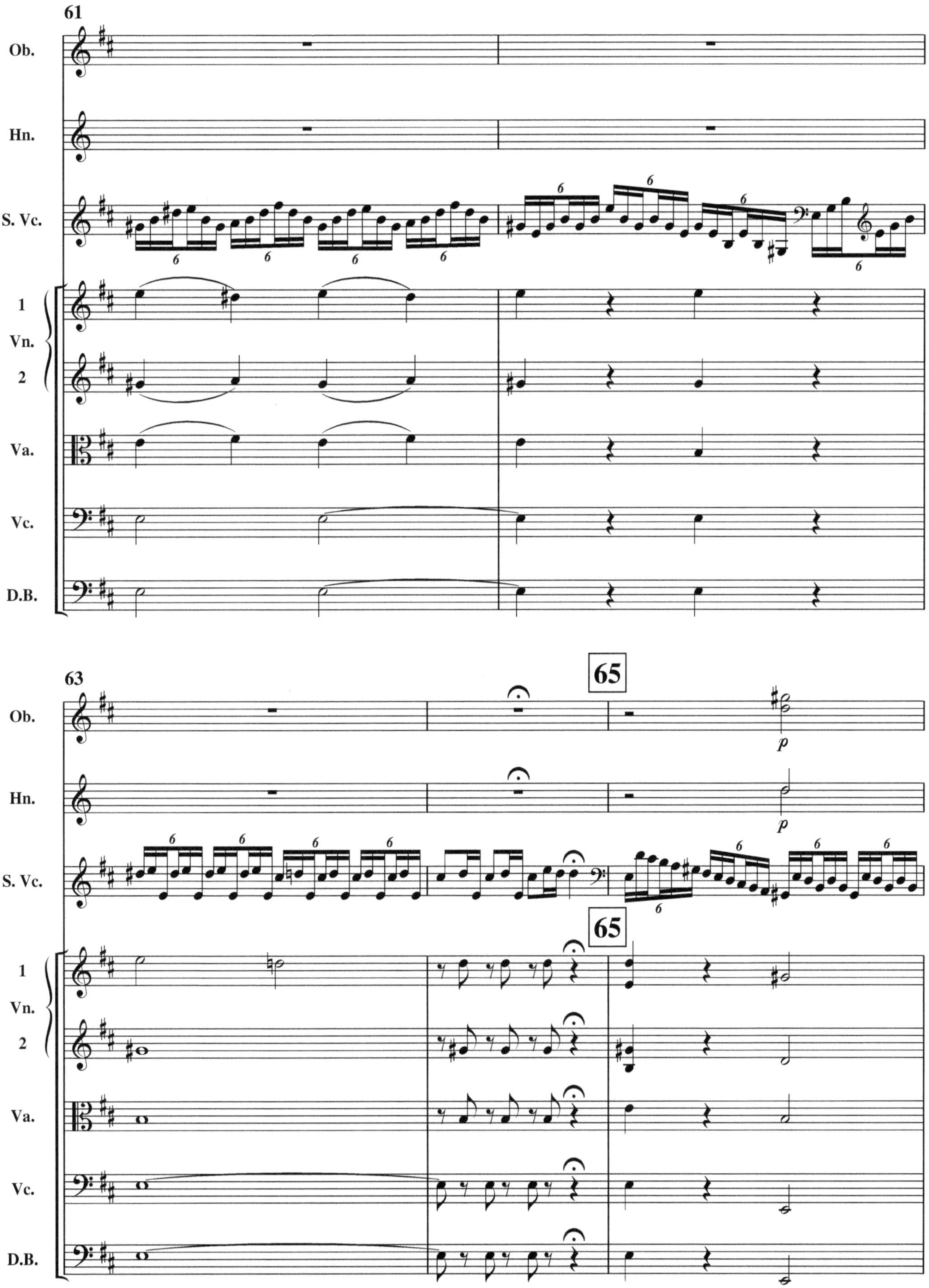
61
Ob.
Hn.
S. Vc.
1
Vn.
2
Va.
Vc.
D.B.
63
65
p
p
65

12

42455

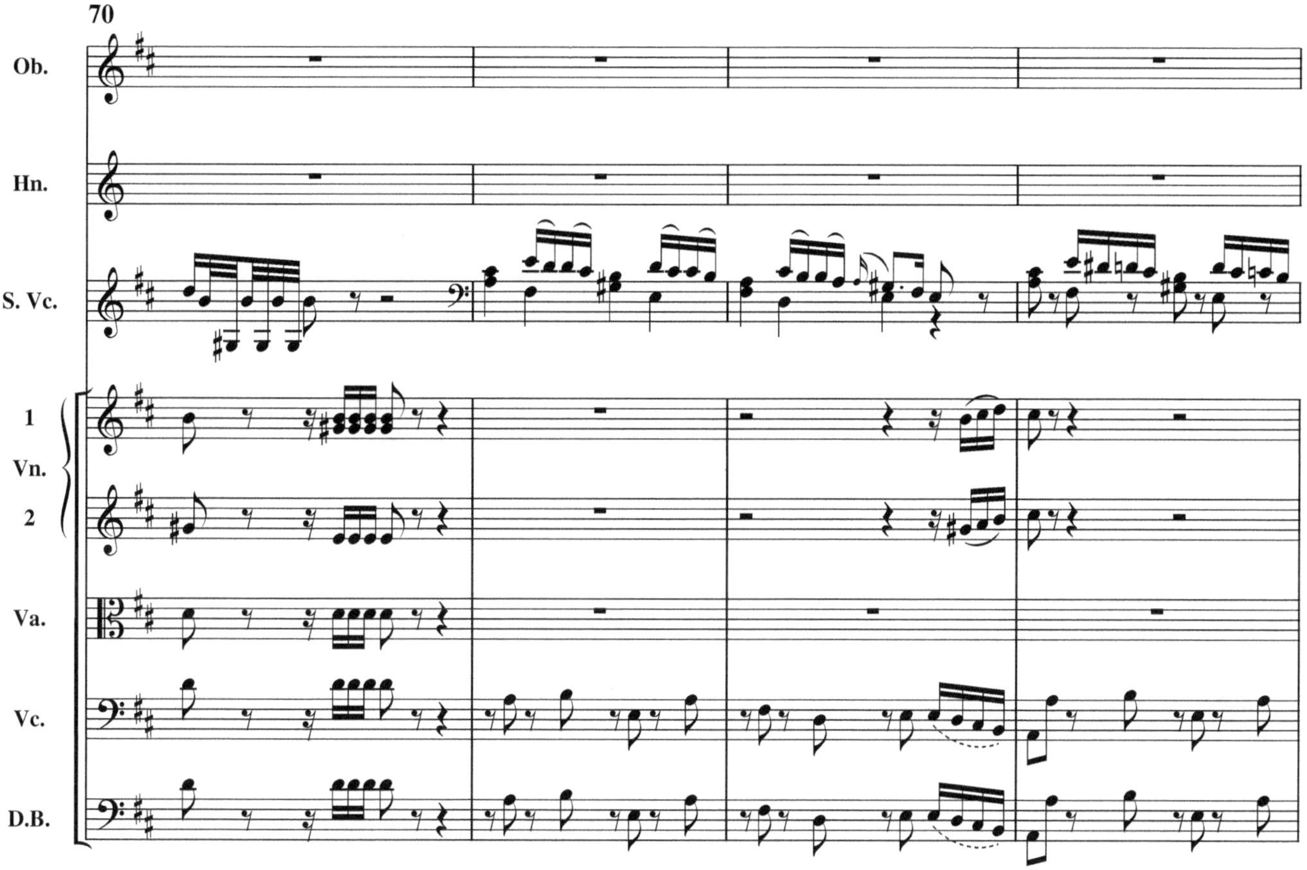
70
Ob.
Hn.
S. Vc.
1
Vn.
2
Va.
Vc.
D.B.

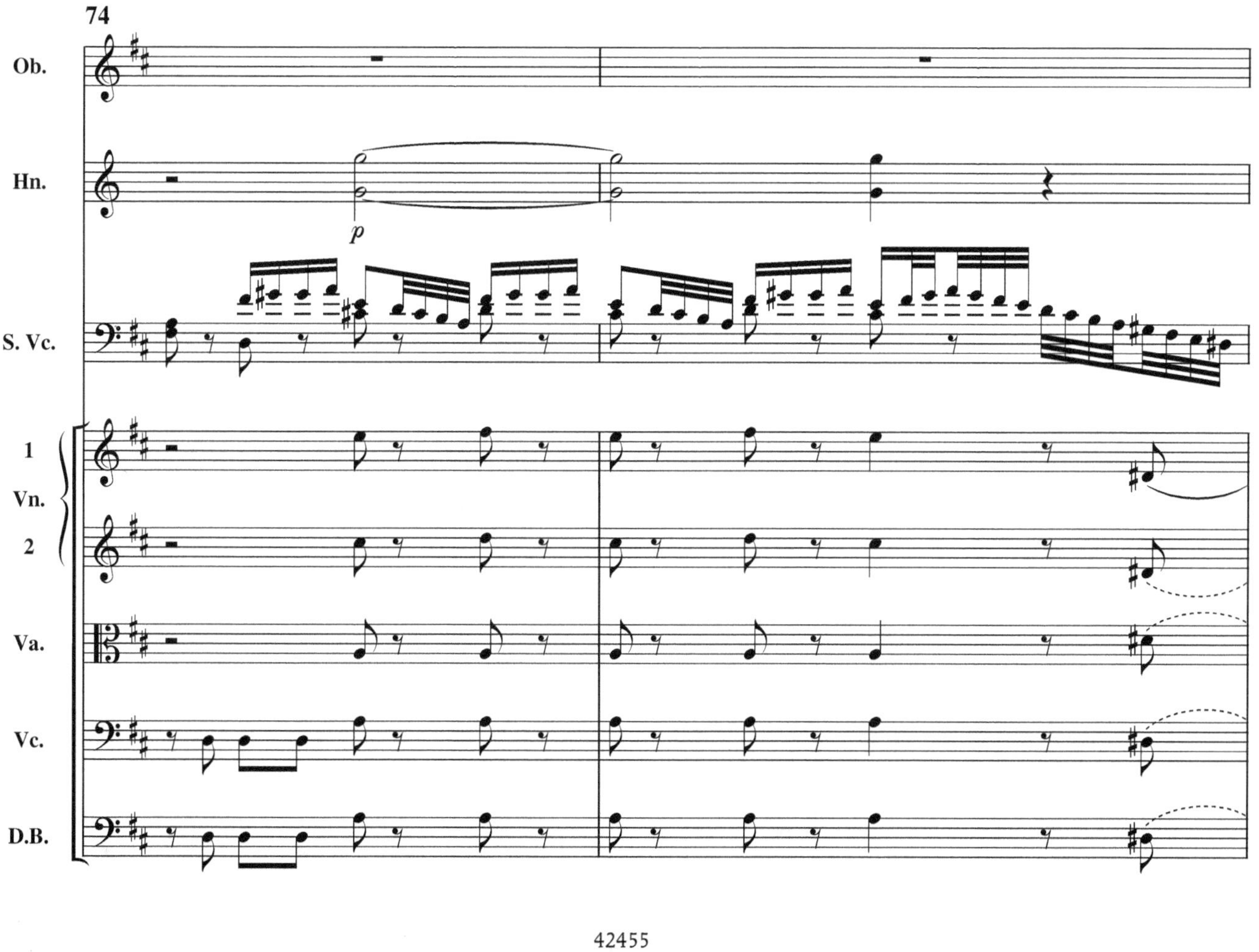
74
Ob.
Hn.
p
S. Vc.
1
Vn.
2
Va.
Vc.
D.B.

14

42455

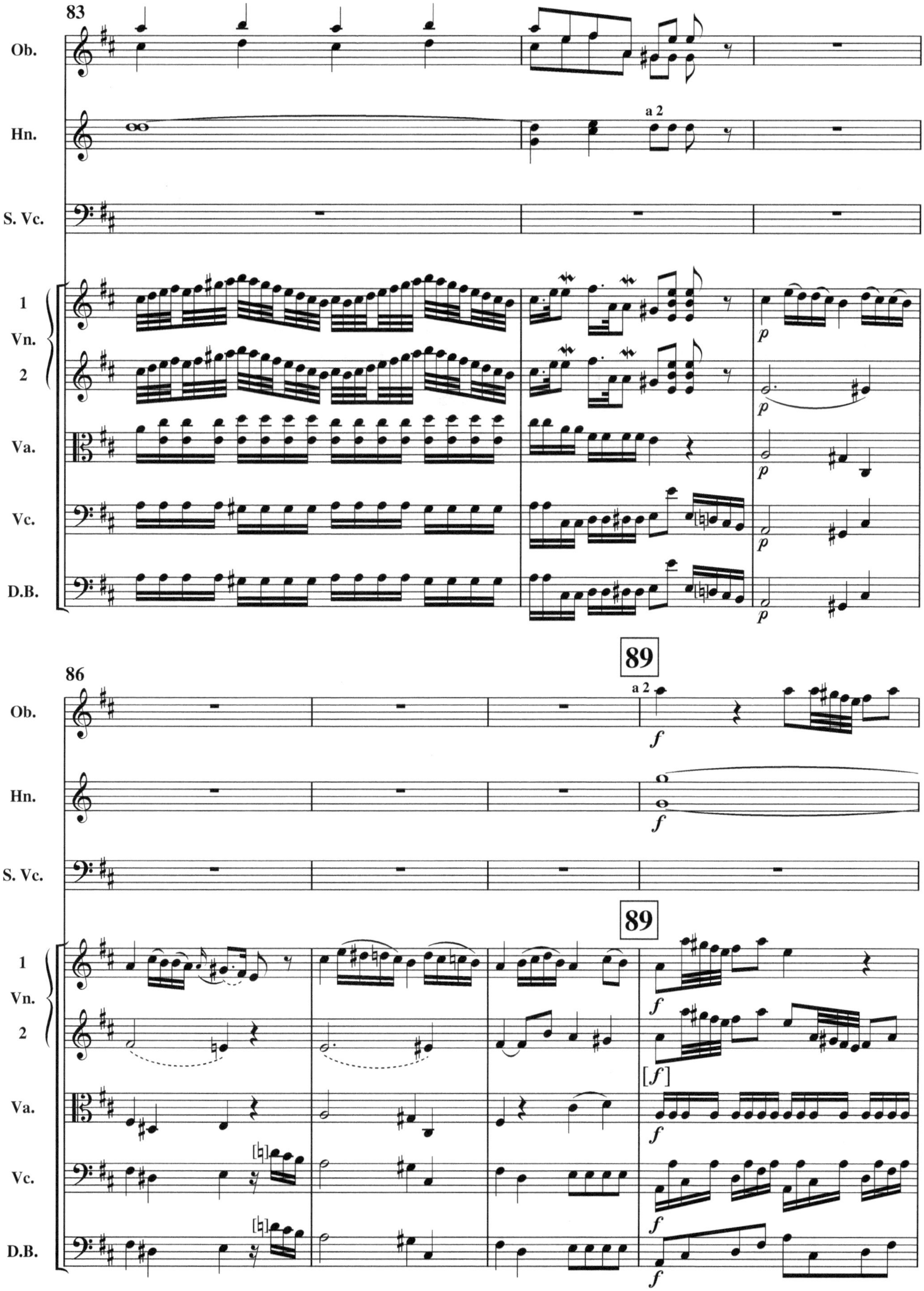
83
Ob.
Hn.
a 2
S. Vc.
1
Vn.
2
Va.
Vc.
D.B.
p
86
89
a 2
f
[f]
[♮]

16

42455

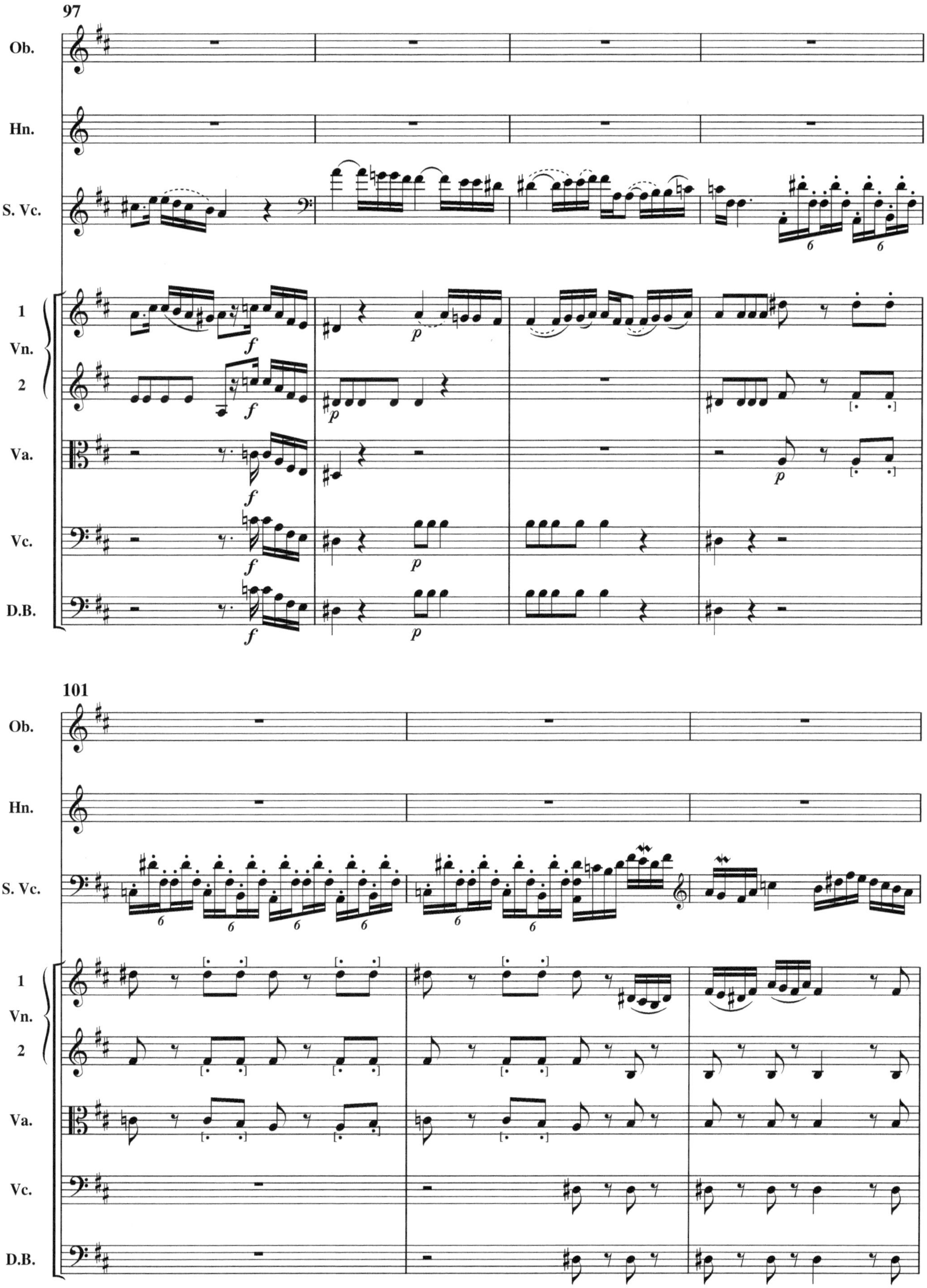
97
Ob.
Hn.
S. Vc.
1
Vn.
2
Va.
Vc.
D.B.
101
Ob.
Hn.
S. Vc.
1
Vn.
2
Va.
Vc.
D.B.

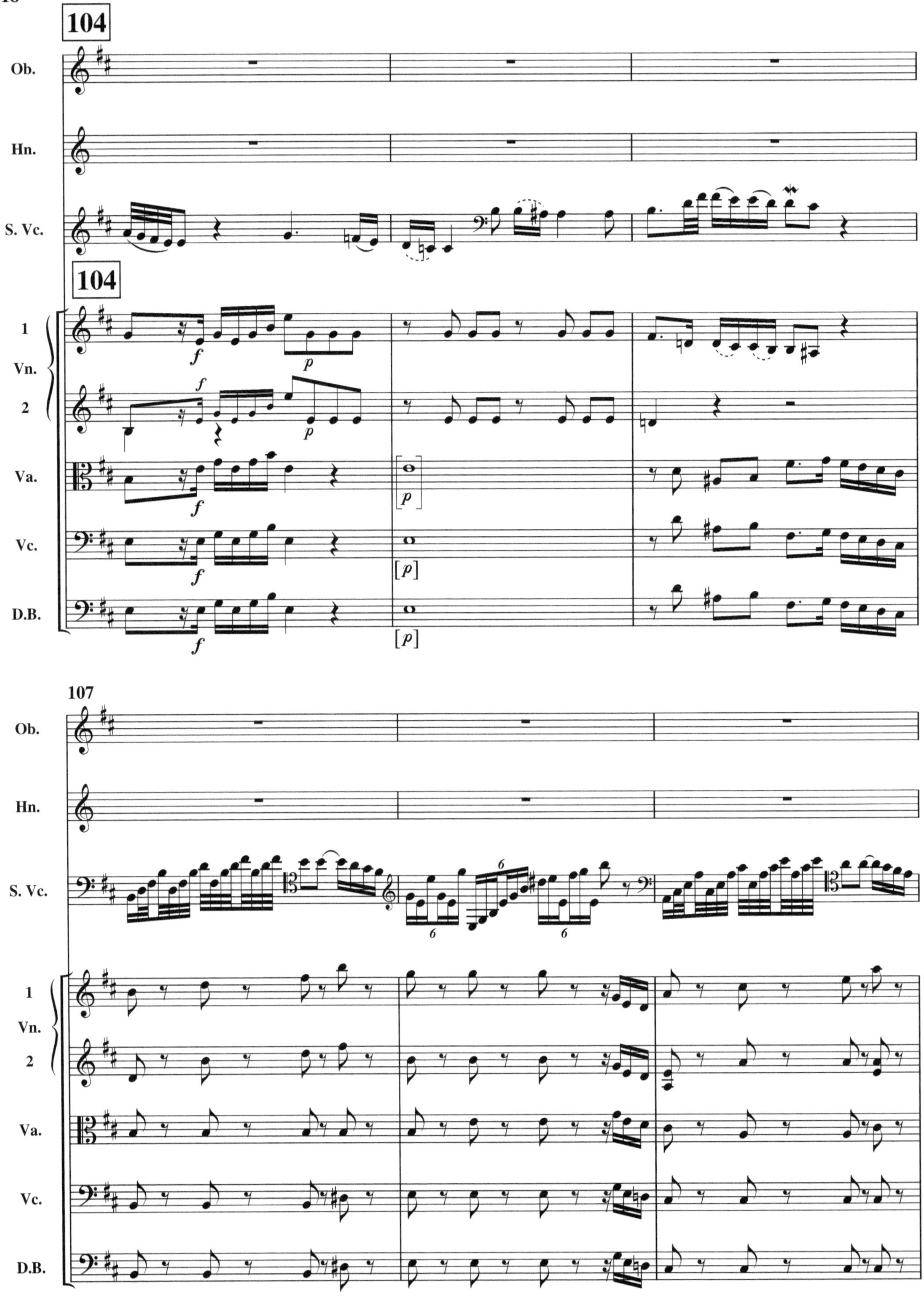
104
Ob.
Hn.
S. Vc.
104
1
Vn.
2
Va.
Vc.
D.B.
f
p
[p]
107
Ob.
Hn.
S. Vc.
1
Vn.
2
Va.
Vc.
D.B.

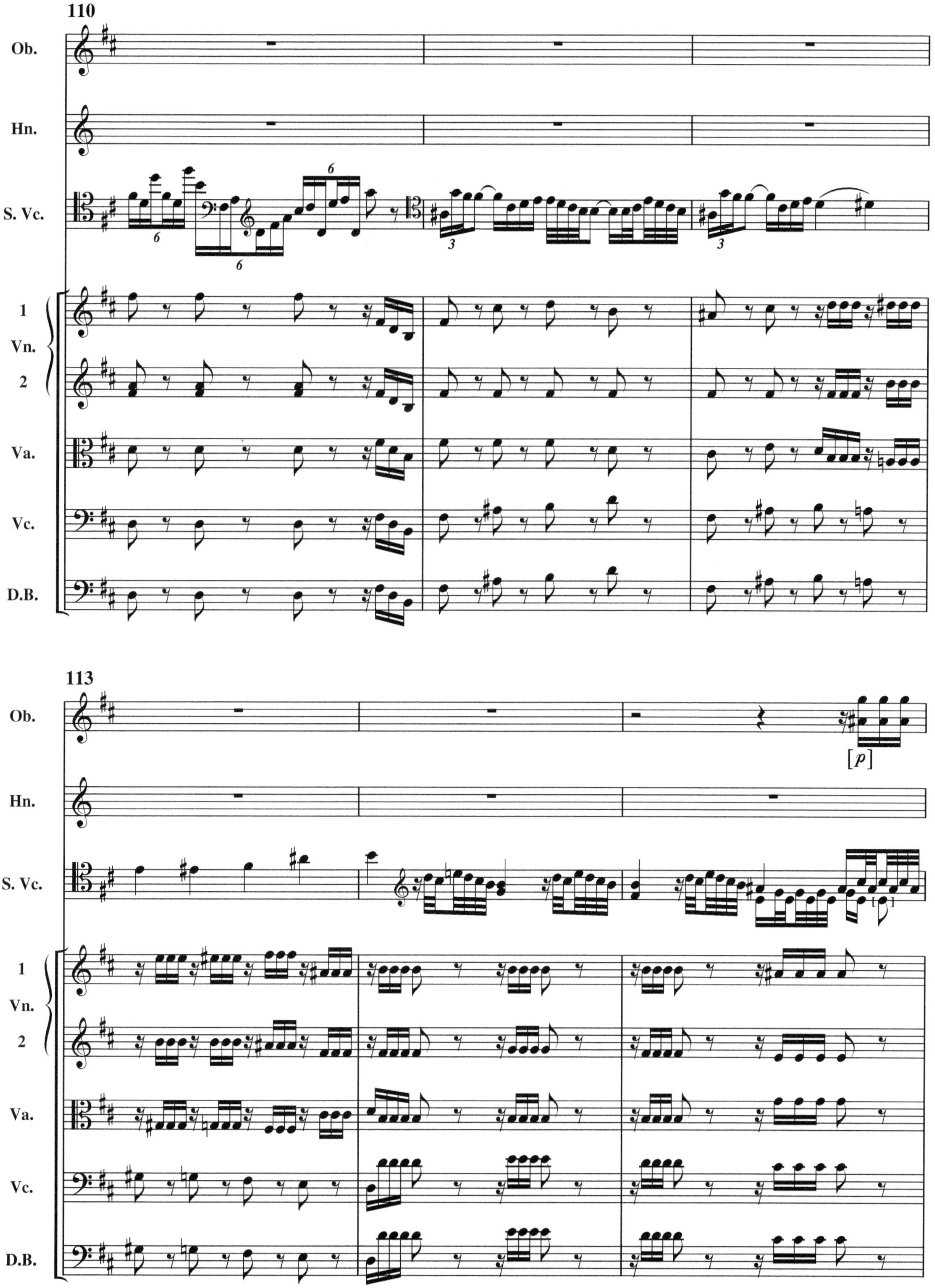
110
Ob.
Hn.
S. Vc.
6
6
6
3
3
1
Vn.
2
Va.
Vc.
D.B.
113
Ob.
[p]
Hn.
S. Vc.
1
Vn.
2
Va.
Vc.
D.B.

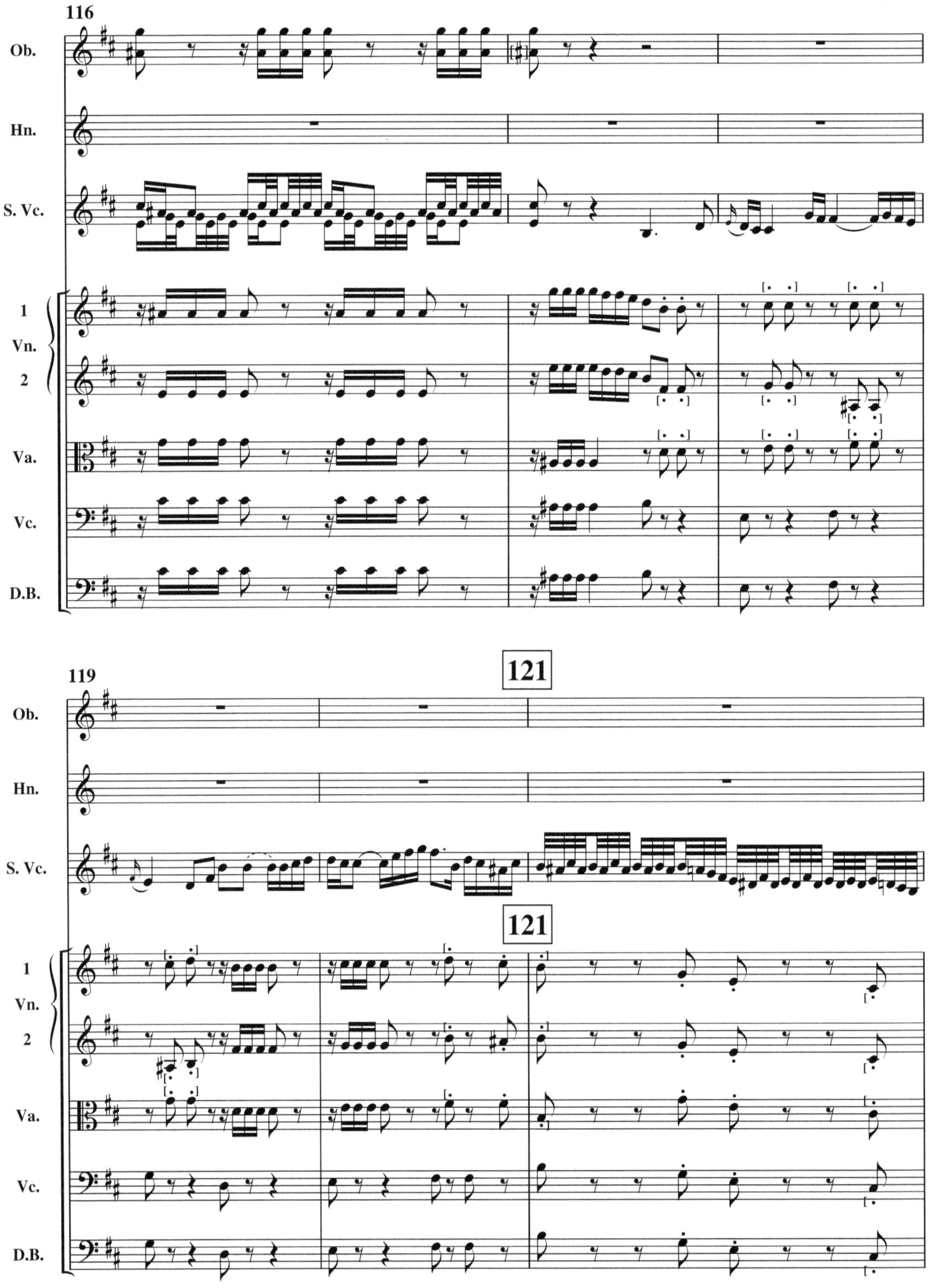
116
Ob.
Hn.
S. Vc.
1
Vn.
2
Va.
Vc.
D.B.
119
121
Ob.
Hn.
S. Vc.
121
1
Vn.
2
Va.
Vc.
D.B.

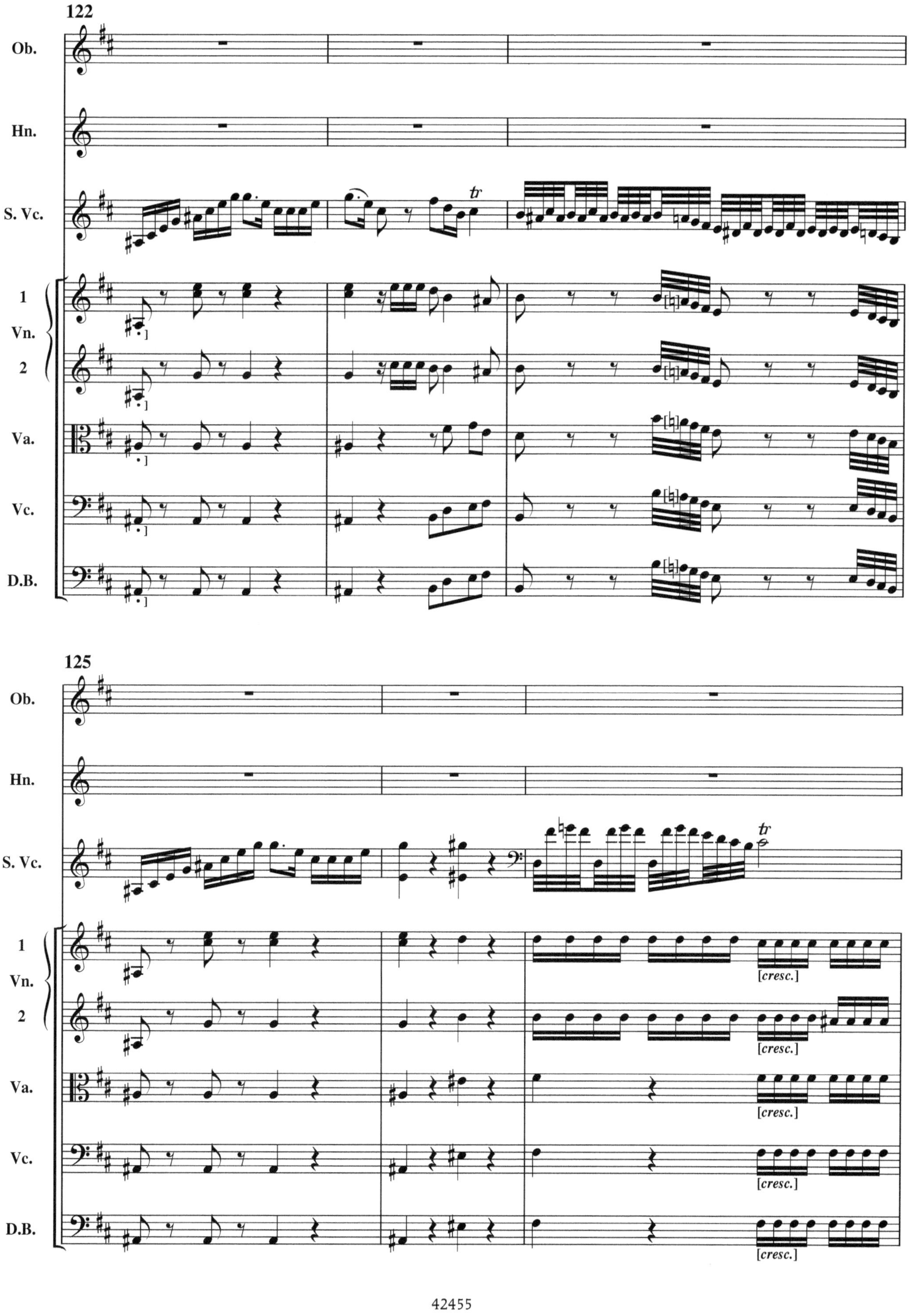
122
Ob.
Hn.
S. Vc.
tr
1
Vn.
2
Va.
Vc.
D.B.
125
Ob.
Hn.
S. Vc.
tr
1
Vn.
2
Va.
Vc.
D.B.
[cresc.]

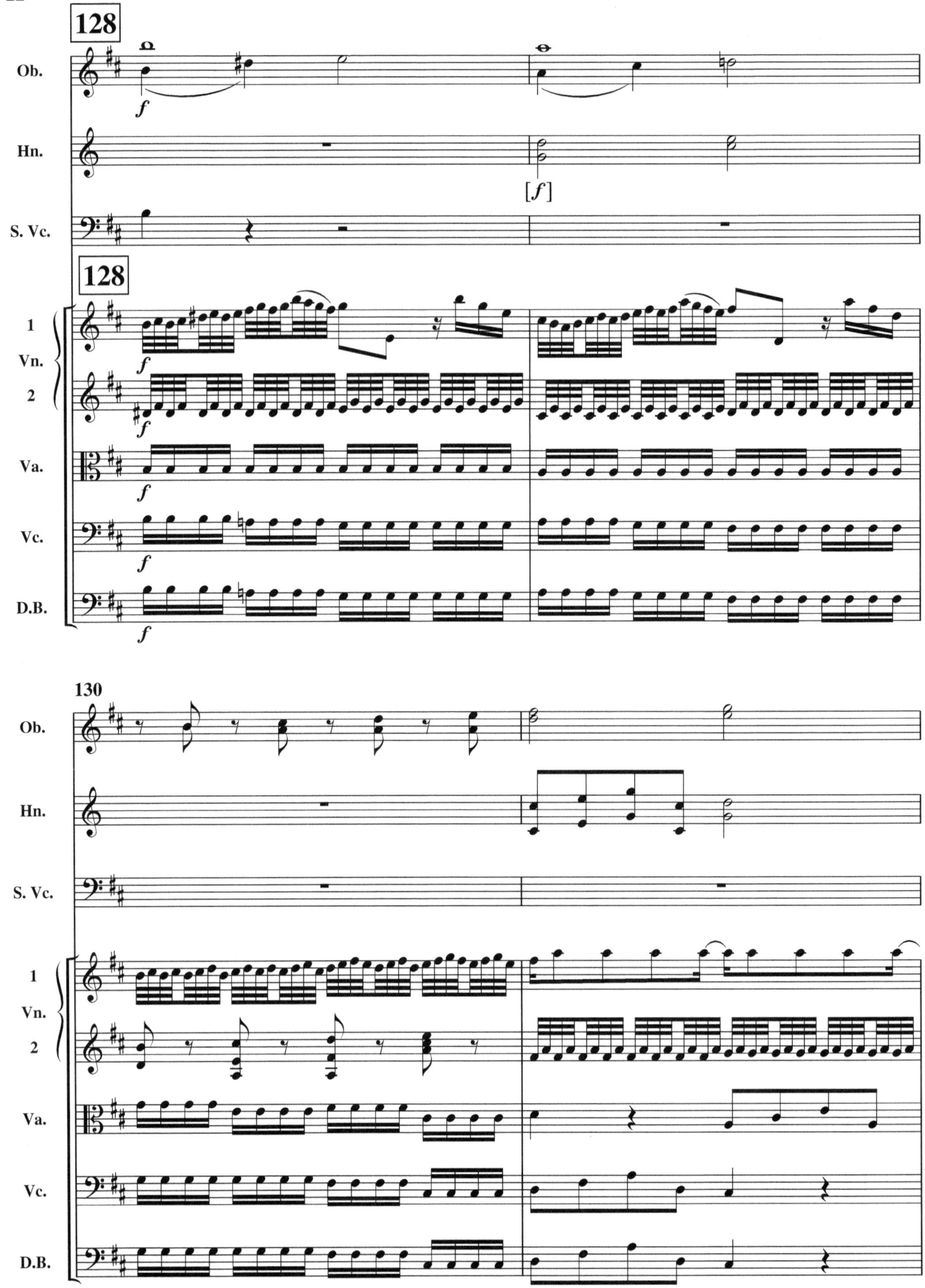
128
Ob.
Hn.
[f]
S. Vc.
128
1
Vn.
2
Va.
Vc.
D.B.
130
Ob.
Hn.
S. Vc.
1
Vn.
2
Va.
Vc.
D.B.

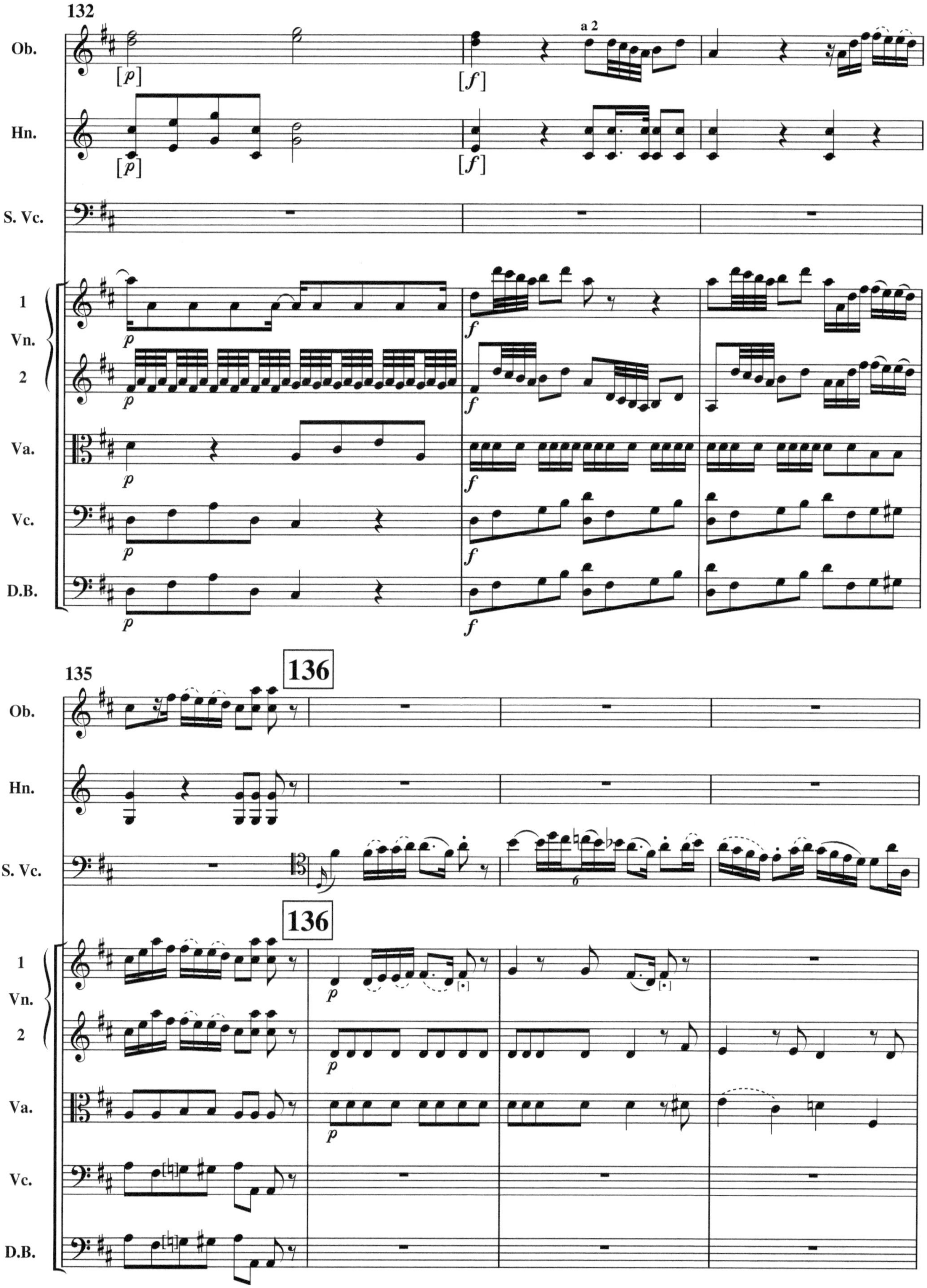
132
Ob.
Hn.
S. Vc.
1
Vn.
2
Va.
Vc.
D.B.
a 2
[p]
[f]
p
f
135
136
136
6

24

42455

145
147
a 2
[f]
6
[p]
[f]
Ob.
Hn.
S. Vc.
1
Vn.
2
Va.
Vc.
D.B.
f
[p]

148
Ob.
Hn.
S. Vc.
1
Vn.
2
Va.
Vc.
D.B.

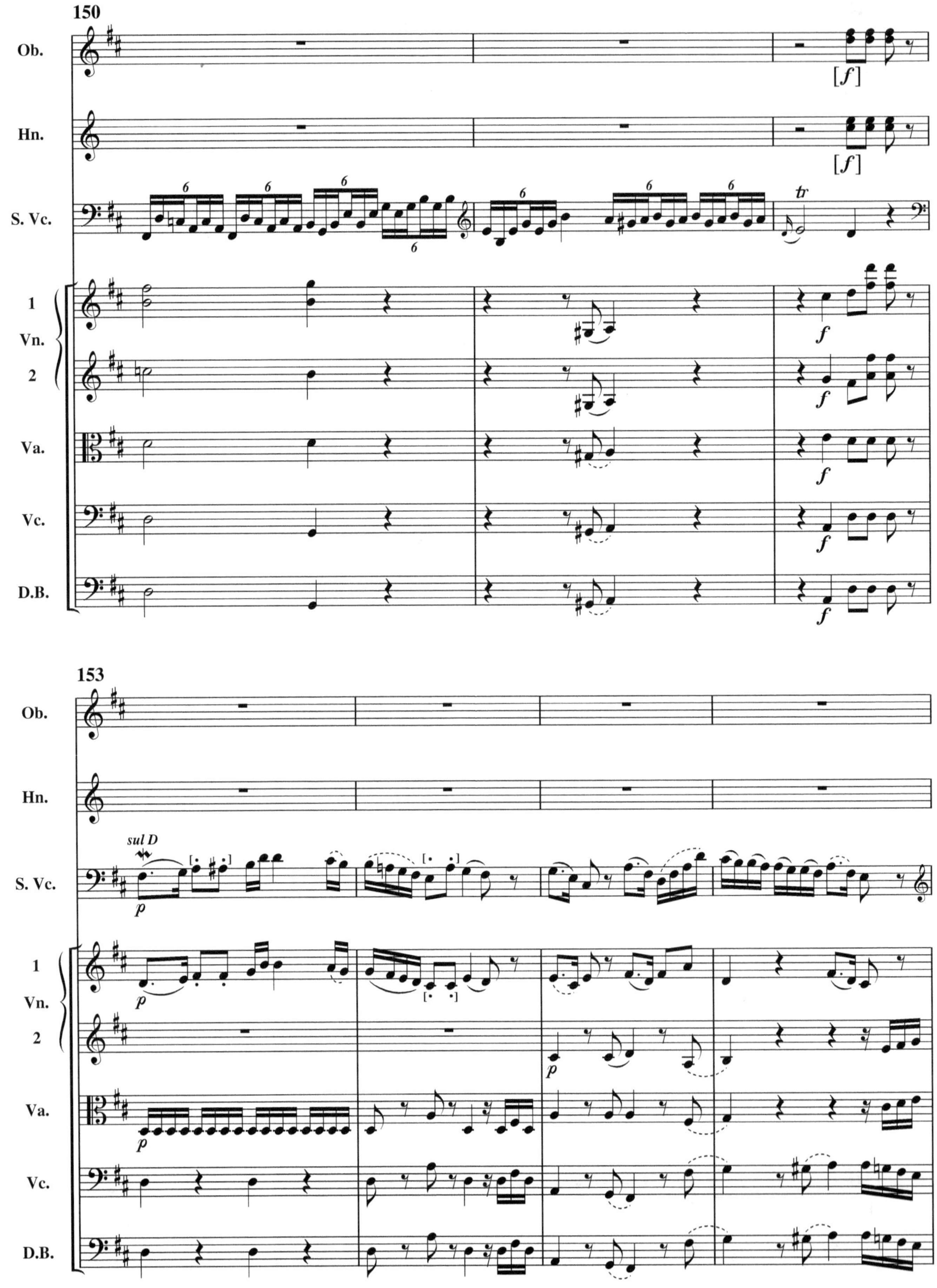
150
Ob.
Hn.
S. Vc.
1
Vn.
2
Va.
Vc.
D.B.
153
Ob.
Hn.
S. Vc.
sul D
1
Vn.
2
Va.
Vc.
D.B.

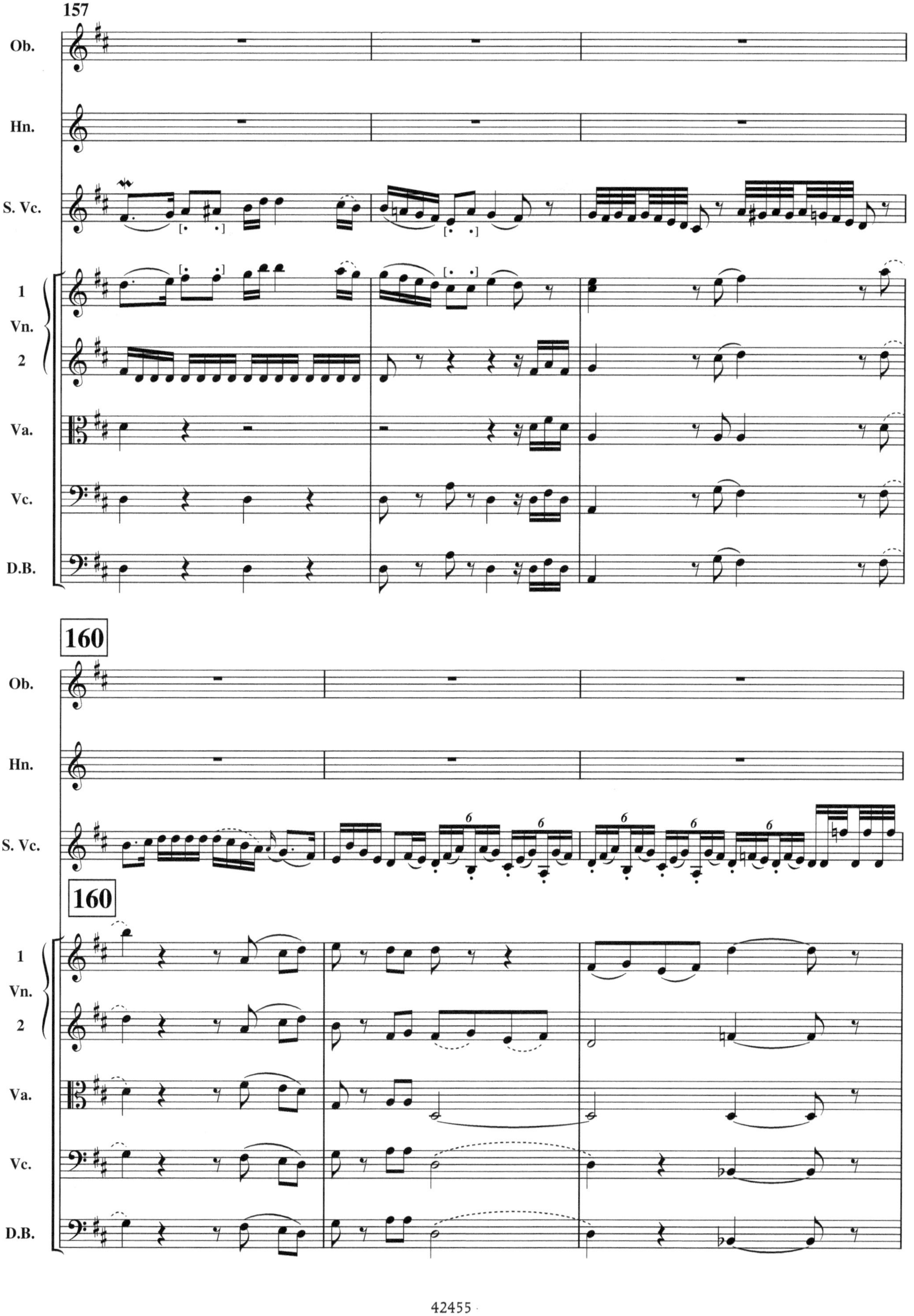
157
Ob.
Hn.
S. Vc.
1
Vn.
2
Va.
Vc.
D.B.
160
Ob.
Hn.
S. Vc.
6
160
1
Vn.
2
Va.
Vc.
D.B.

28

42455

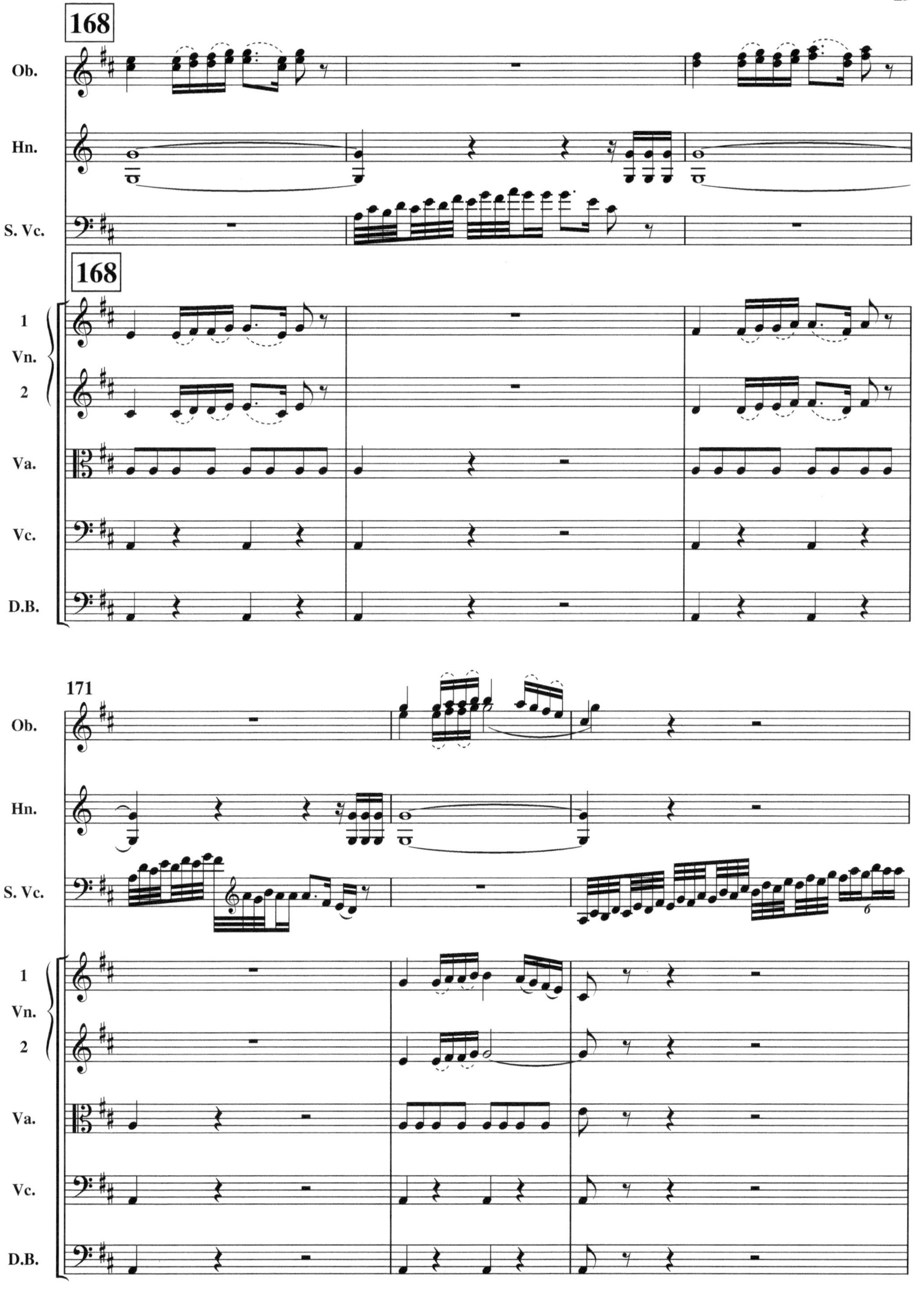
168
Ob.
Hn.
S. Vc.
168
1
Vn.
2
Va.
Vc.
D.B.
171
Ob.
Hn.
S. Vc.
6
1
Vn.
2
Va.
Vc.
D.B.

174
Ob.
Hn.
S. Vc.
[loco]
6
6
6
1
Vn.
2
Va.
Vc.
D.B.

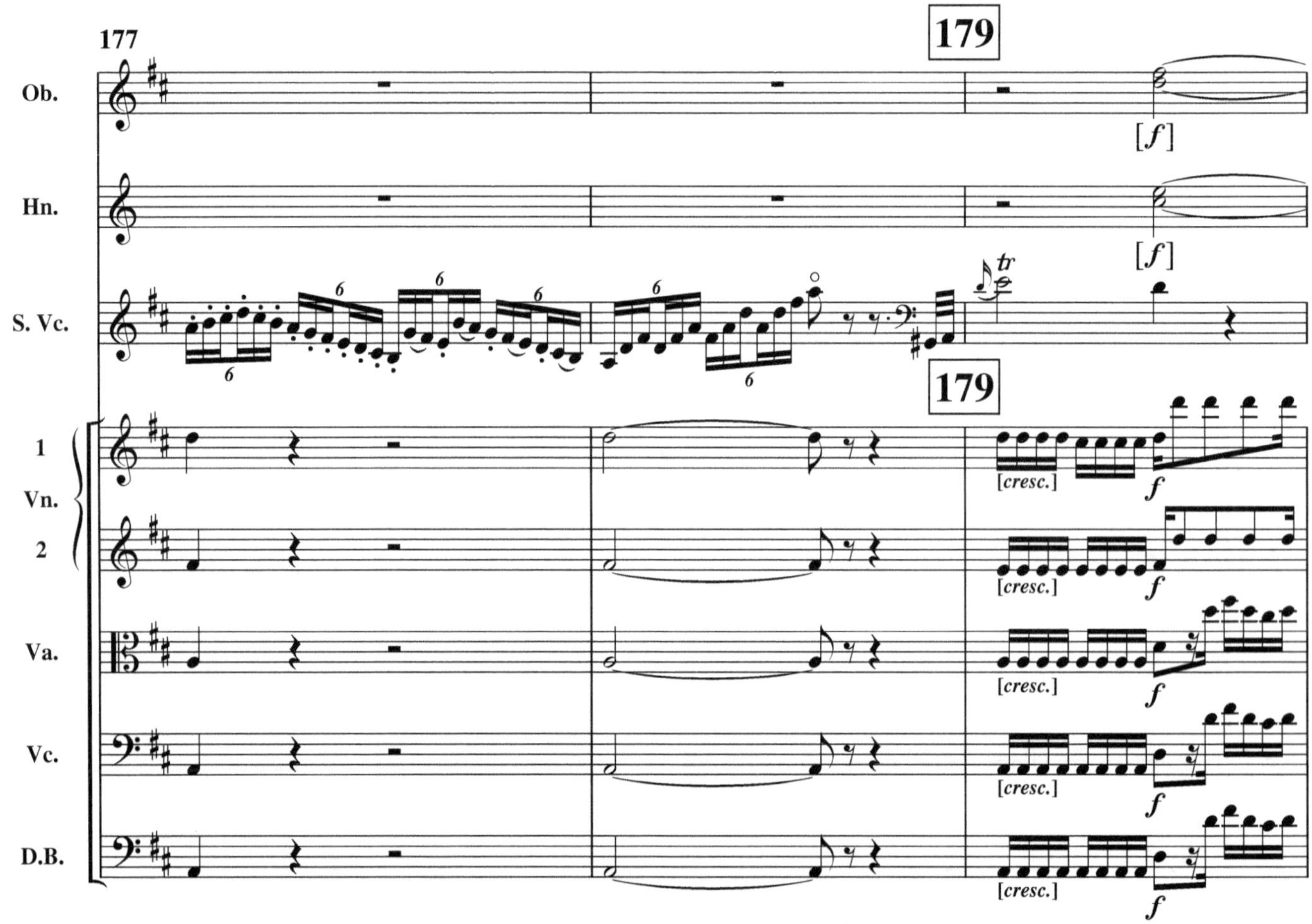
177
179
Ob.
[f]
Hn.
[f]
S. Vc.
6
6
6
6
6
tr
179
1
Vn.
2
[cresc.]
f
[cresc.]
f
Va.
[cresc.]
f
Vc.
[cresc.]
f
D.B.
[cresc.]
f

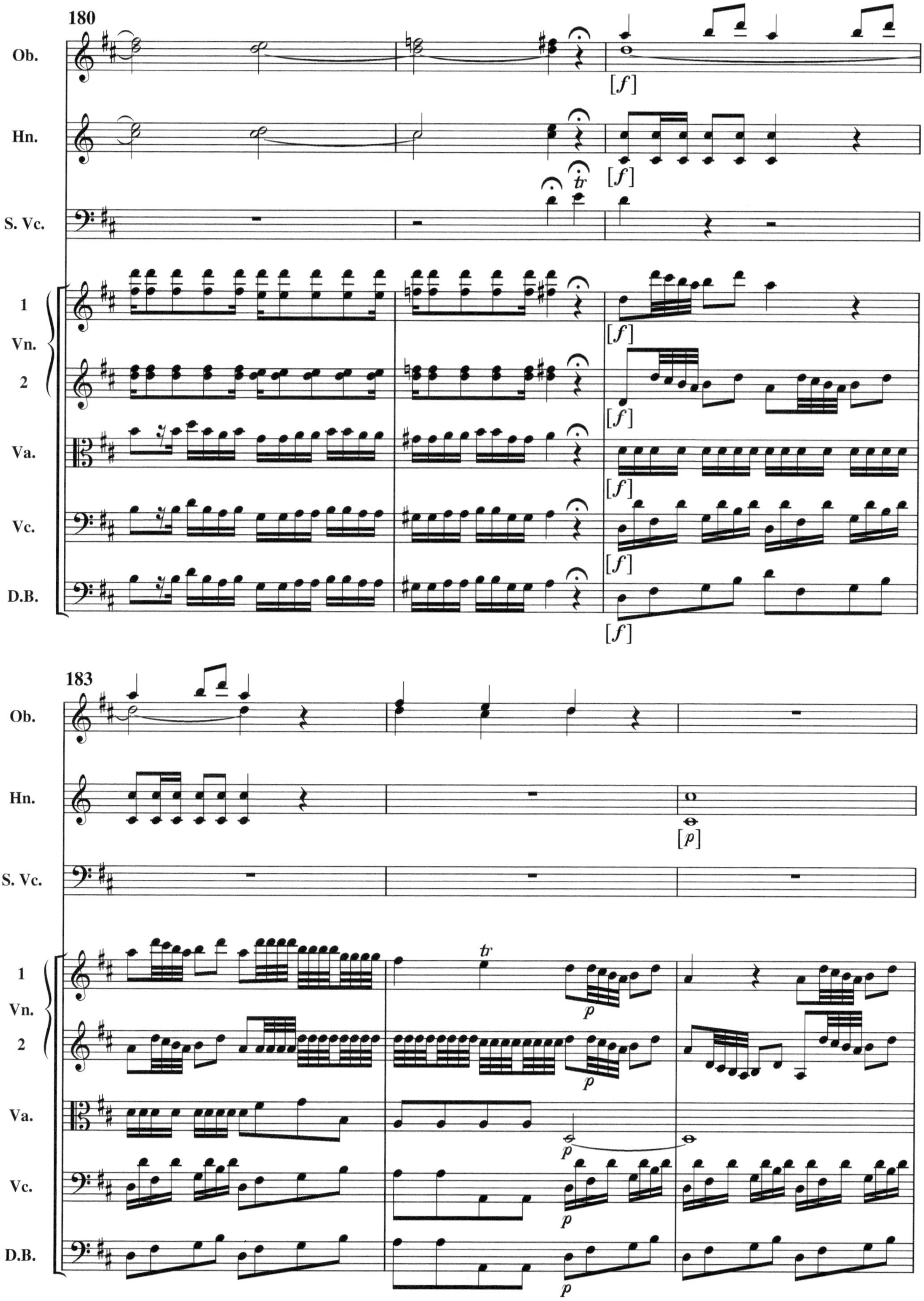
180
Ob.
Hn.
S. Vc.
1
Vn.
2
Va.
Vc.
D.B.
[f]
tr
183
[p]
p

32

42455

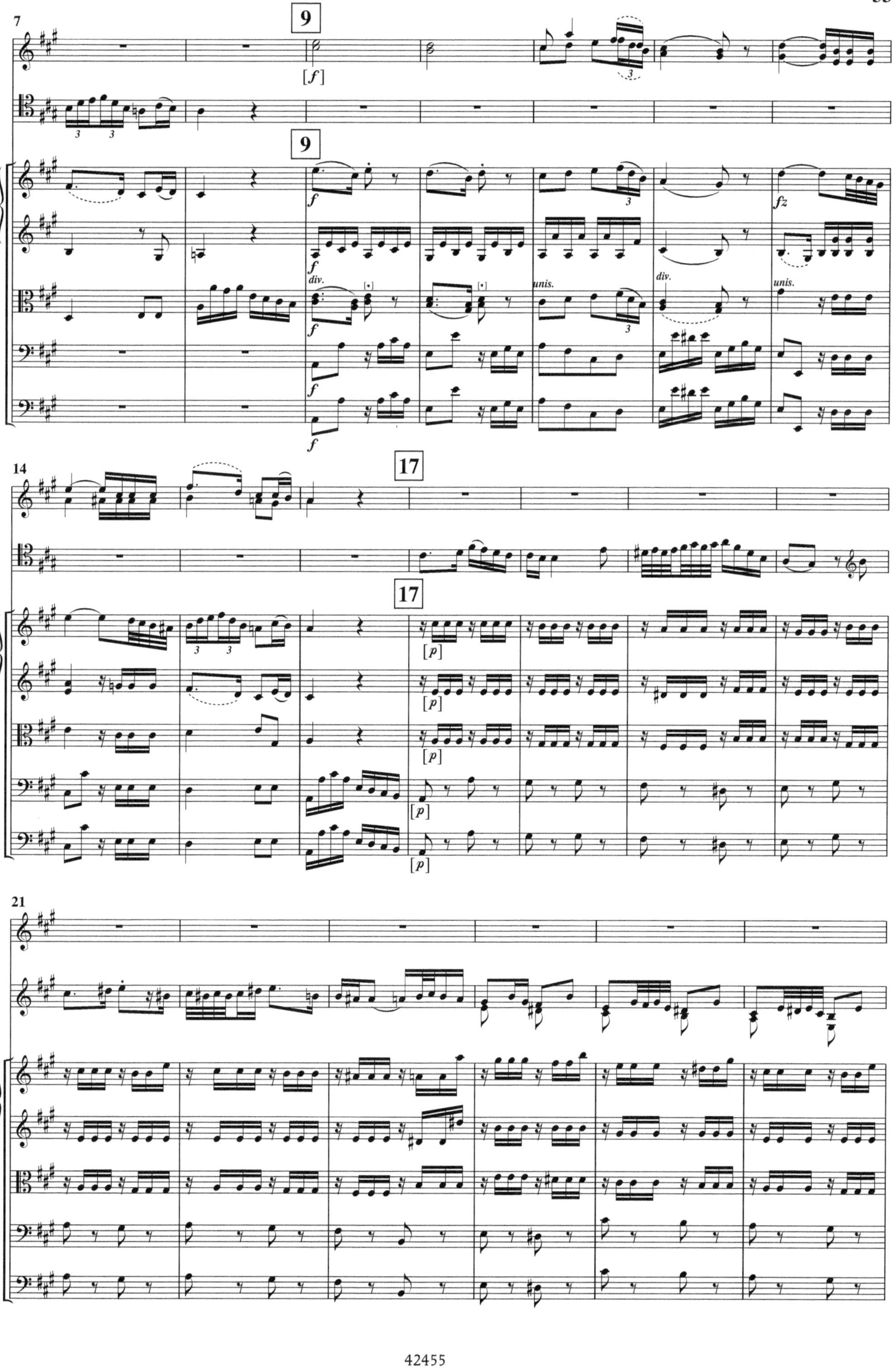
7
9
Ob.
S. Vc.
1
Vn.
2
Va.
Vc.
D.B.
[f]
f
fz
div.
unis.
14
17
[p]
21

27
32
Ob.
S. Vc.
32
1
Vn.
2
Va.
Vc.
D.B.
34
Ob.
S. Vc.
3 3
f
1
Vn.
2
Va.
Vc.
D.B.
40
43
Ob.
S. Vc.
43
1
Vn.
2
Va.
Vc.
D.B.
p

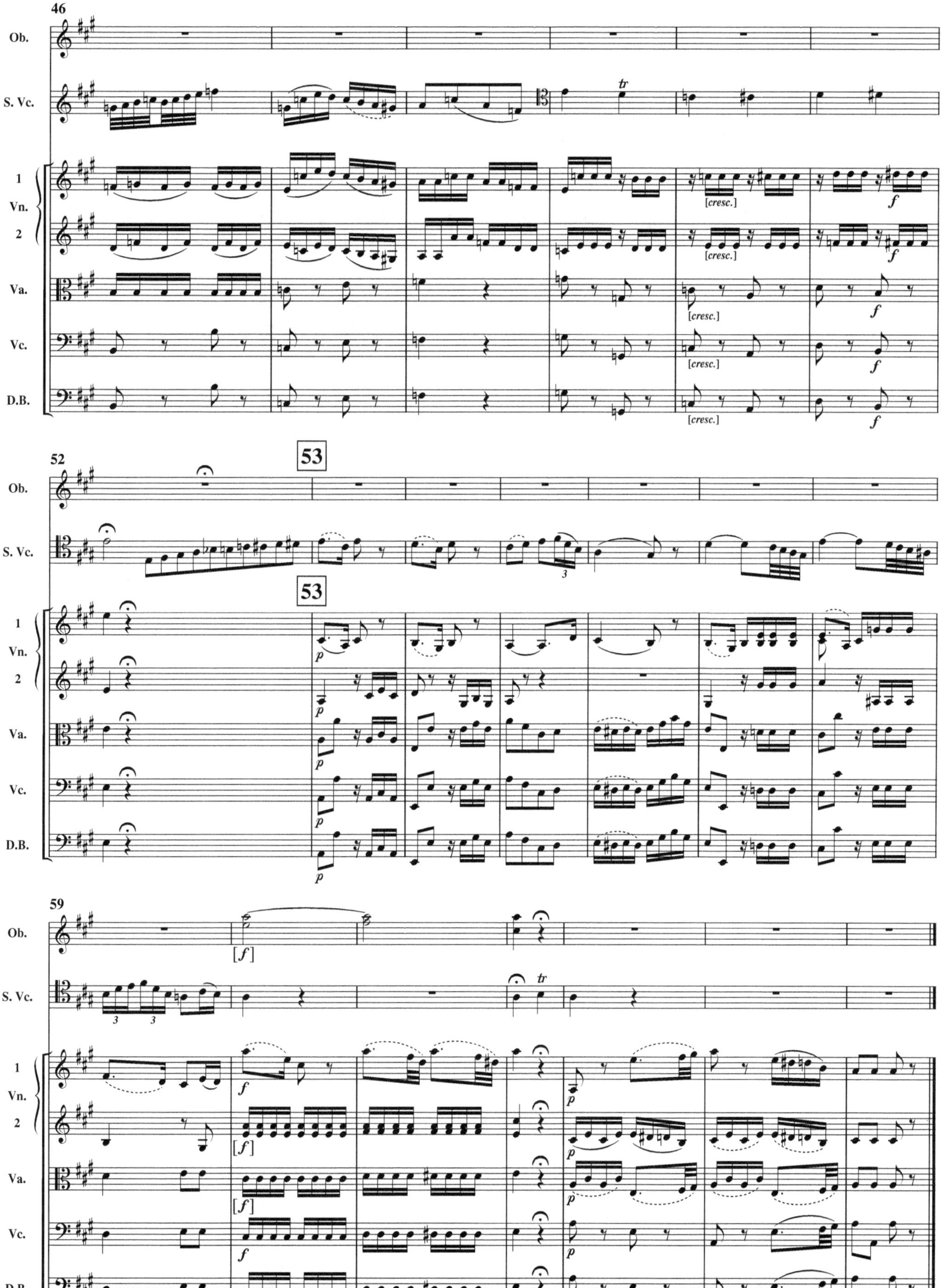
46
Ob.
S. Vc.
1
Vn.
2
Va.
Vc.
D.B.
tr
[cresc.]
f
52
53
p
59
[f]
f
p
3

Allegro
Ob.
Hn.
S. Vc.
Allegro
1
Vn.
2
Va.
Vc.
D.B.
9
Ob.
Hn.
S. Vc.
9
1
Vn.
2
Va.
Vc.
D.B.

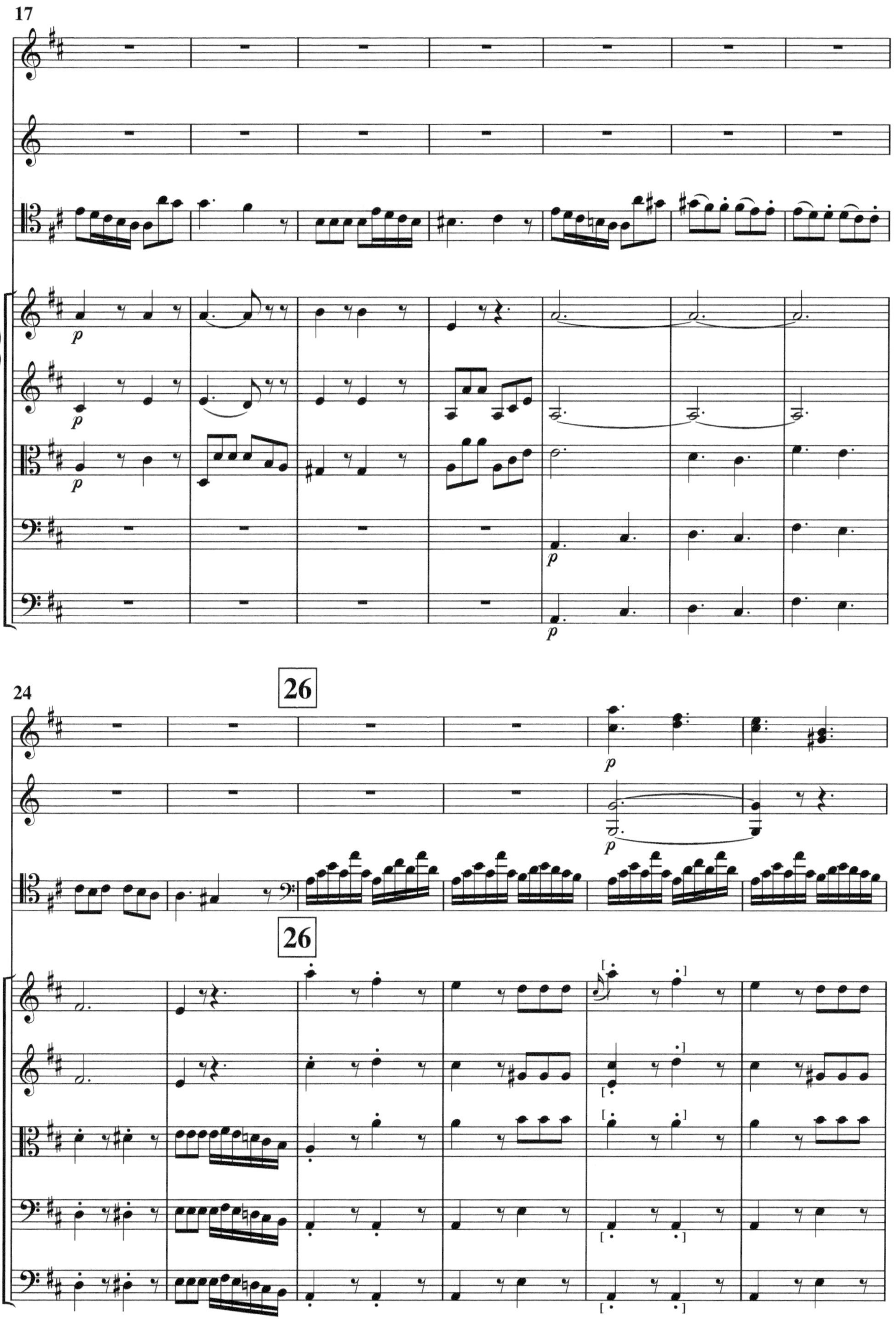
17
Ob.
Hn.
S. Vc.
1
Vn.
2
Va.
Vc.
D.B.
p
24
26
26

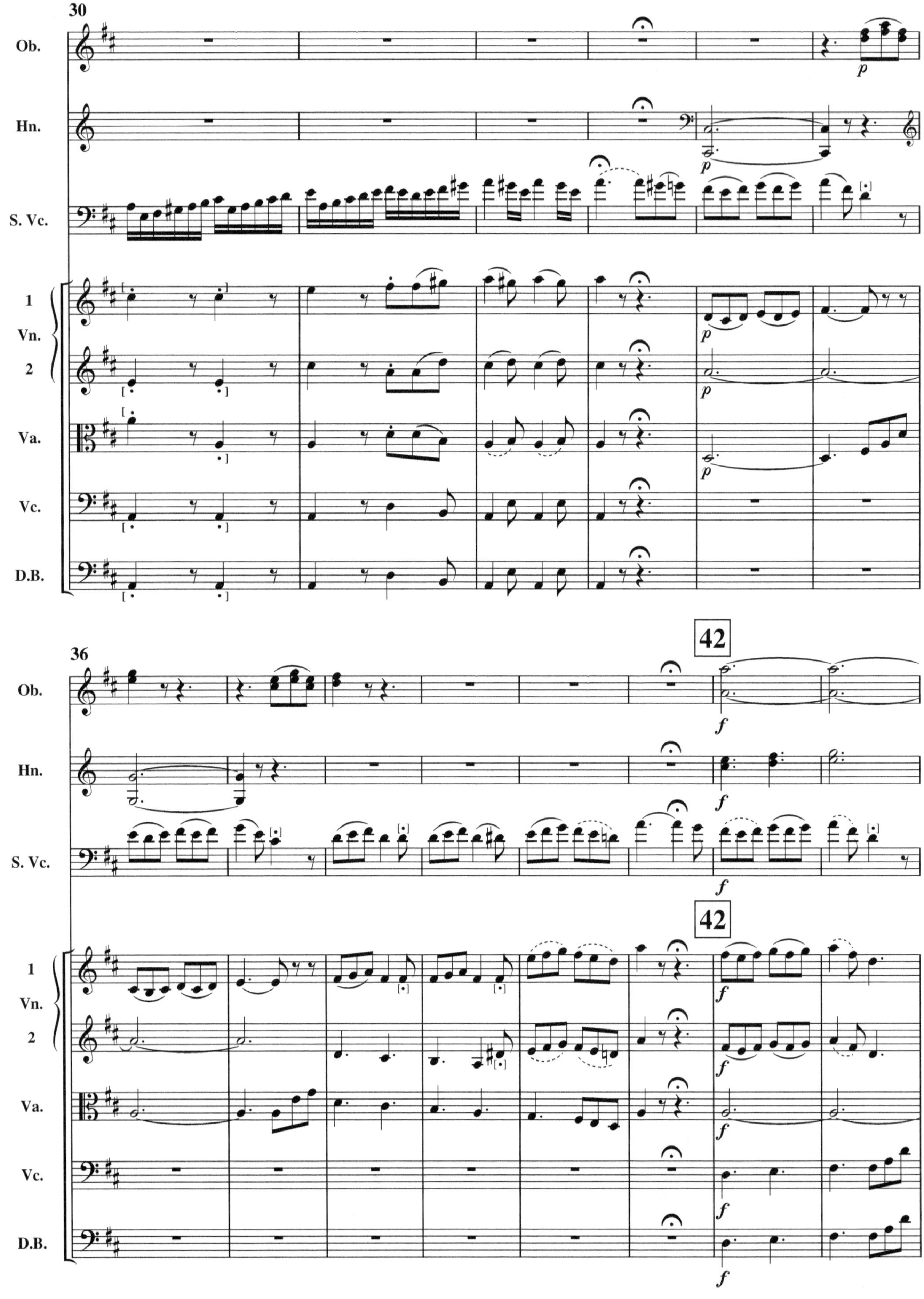
30
Ob.
Hn.
S. Vc.
1
Vn.
2
Va.
Vc.
D.B.
p
36
42
f

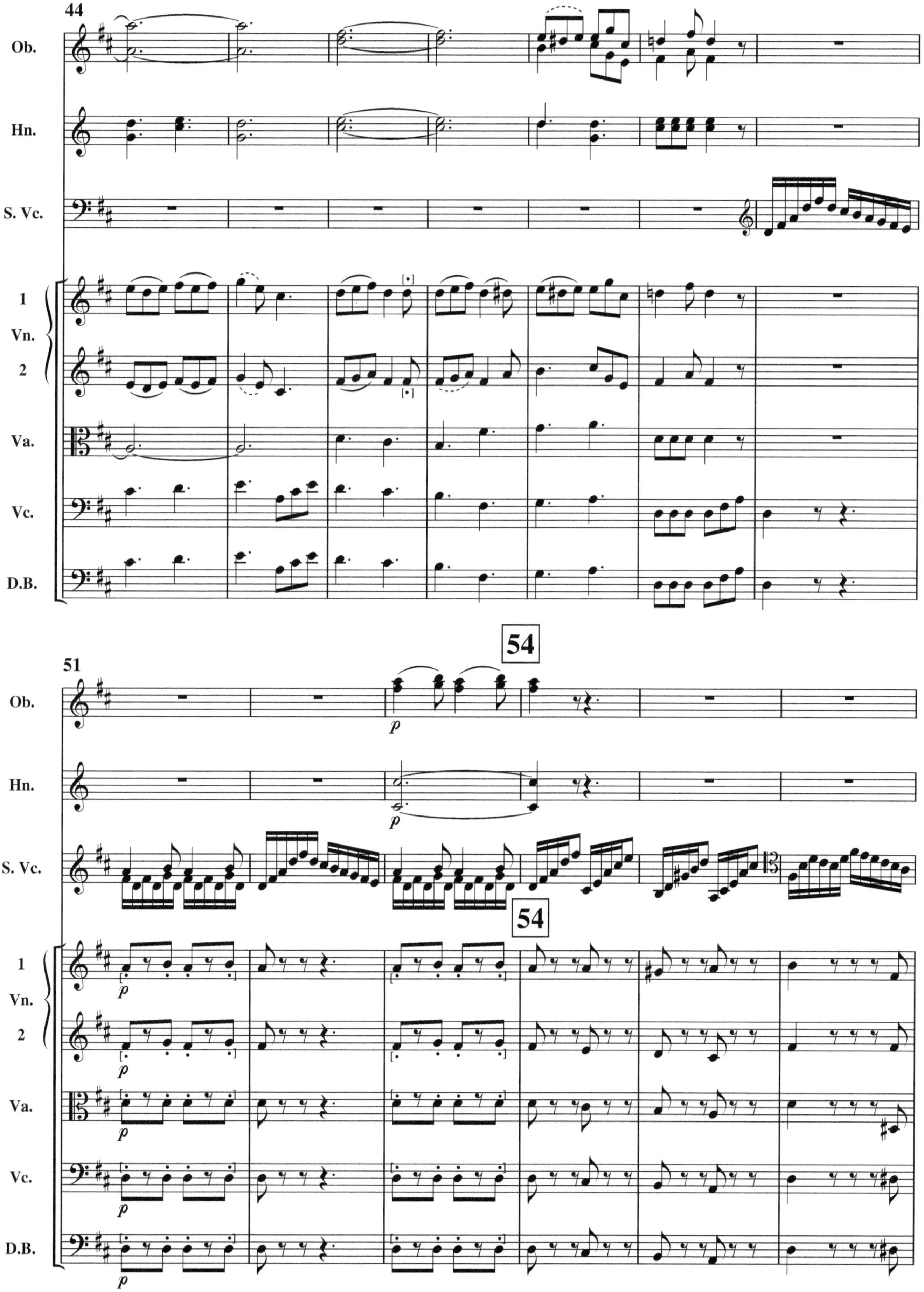
44
Ob.
Hn.
S. Vc.
1
Vn.
2
Va.
Vc.
D.B.
51
54
Ob.
p
Hn.
p
S. Vc.
54
1
Vn.
2
Va.
Vc.
D.B.
p

57
Ob.
Hn.
a 2
[p]
S. Vc.
1
Vn.
2
[p]
[p]
Va.
Vc.
D.B.
64
66
Ob.
[p]
Hn.
[p]
S. Vc.
66
1
Vn.
2
Va.
Vc.
p
D.B.
p

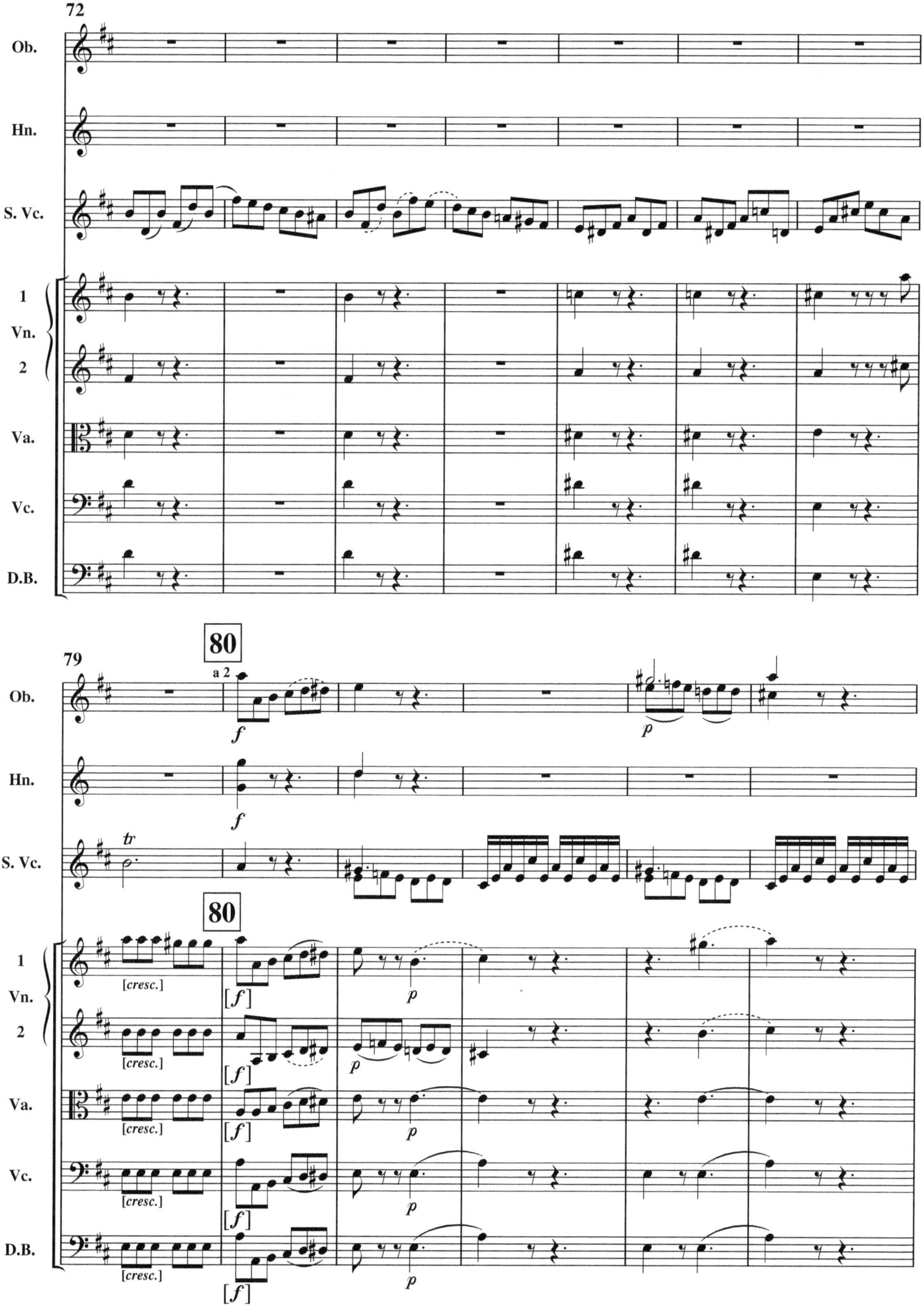
72
Ob.
Hn.
S. Vc.
1
Vn.
2
Va.
Vc.
D.B.
79
80
a 2
f
p
tr
[cresc.]
[f]

42

42455

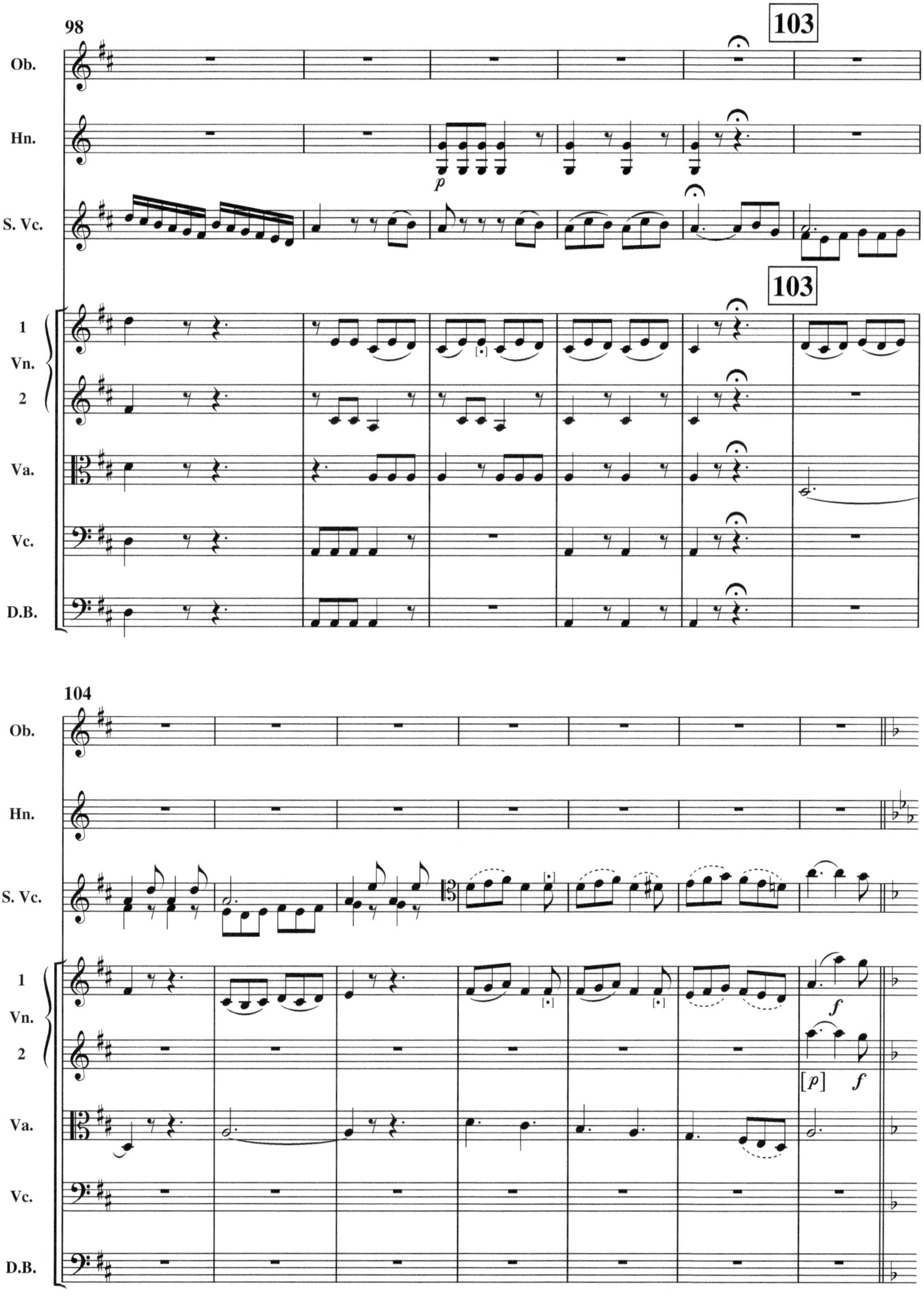
98
103
Ob.
Hn.
S. Vc.
1
Vn.
2
Va.
Vc.
D.B.
p
[•]
104
f
[p]
f

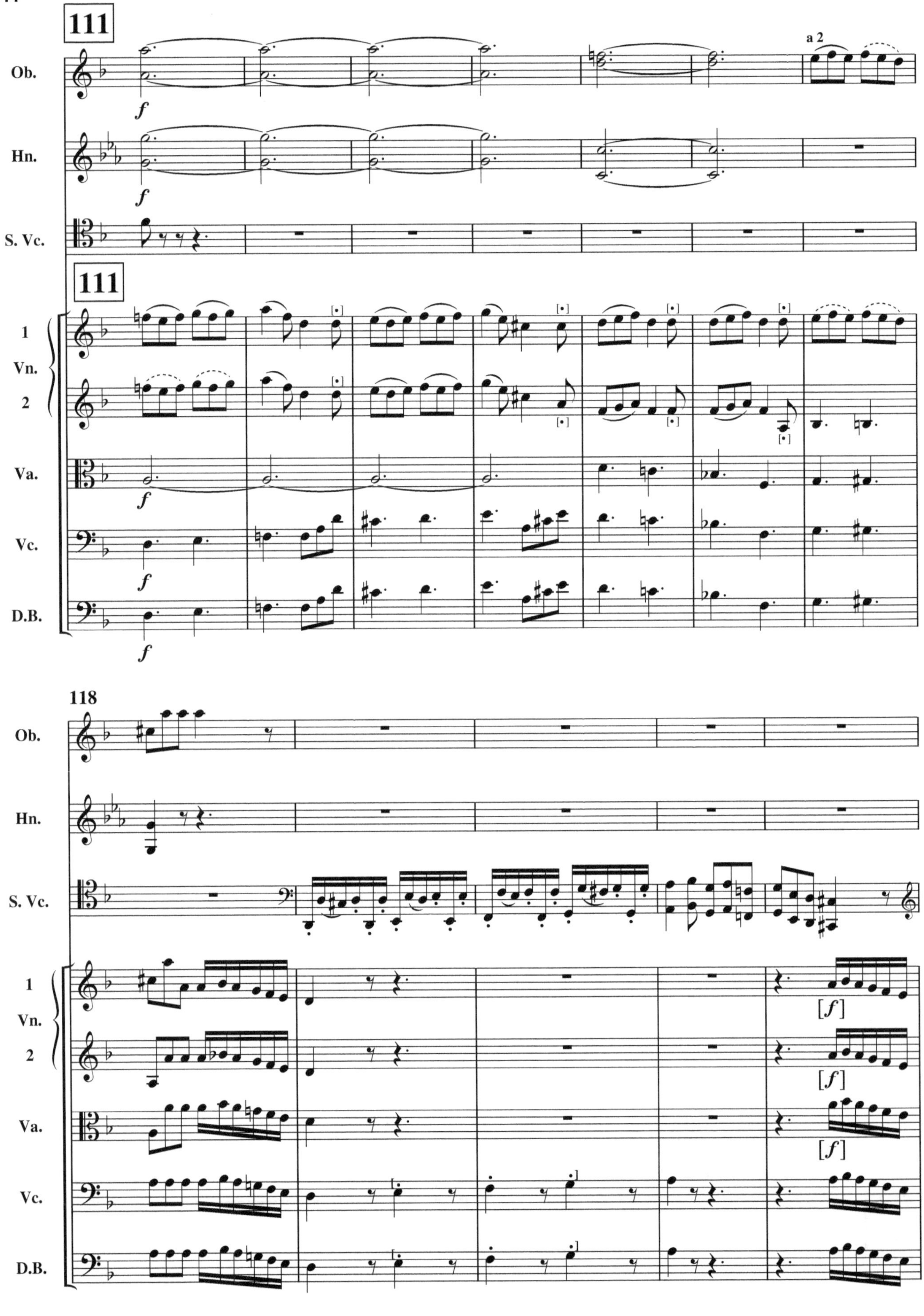
111
Ob.
Hn.
S. Vc.
111
1
Vn.
2
Va.
Vc.
D.B.
a 2
f
118
Ob.
Hn.
S. Vc.
1
Vn.
2
Va.
Vc.
D.B.
[f]

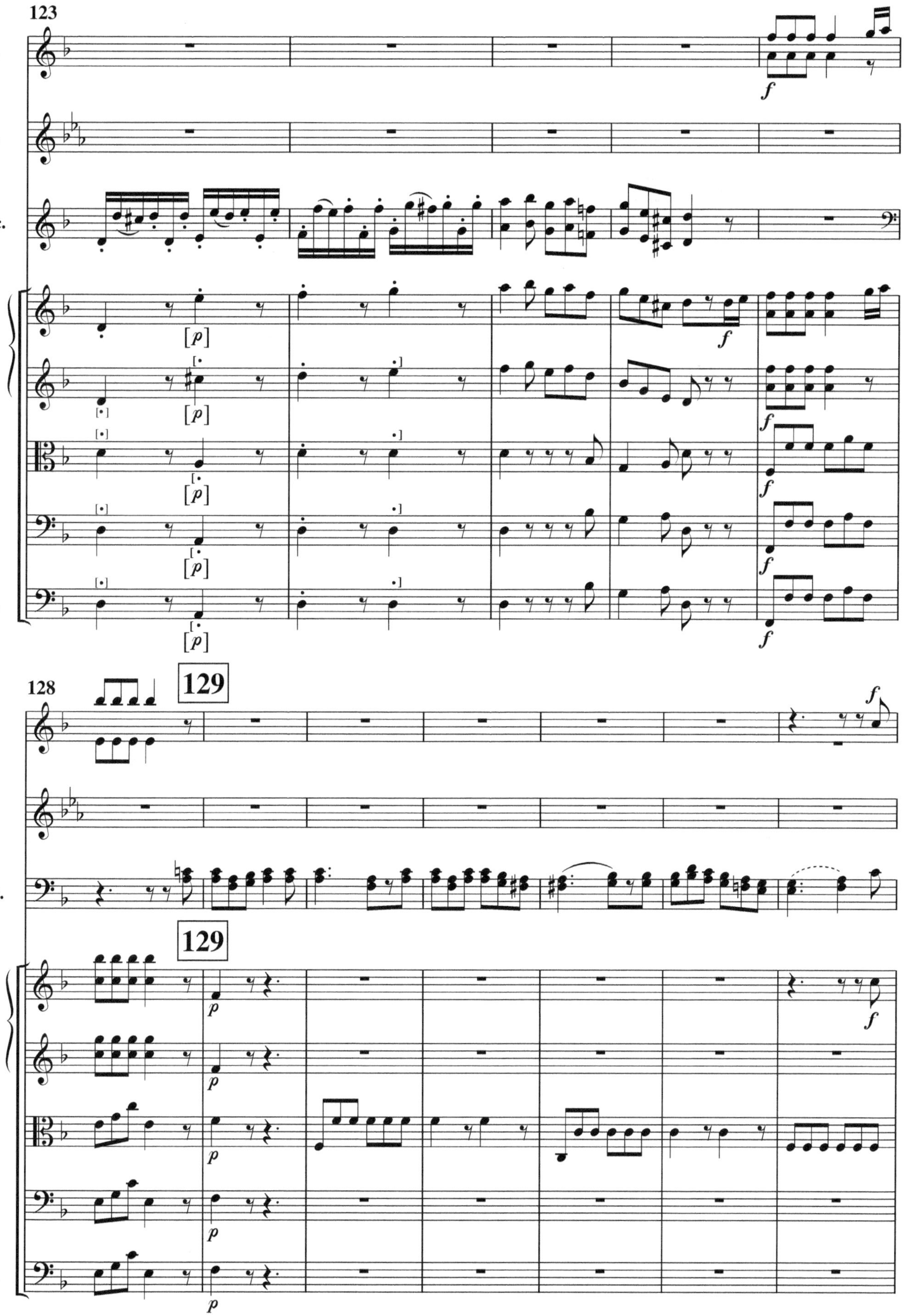
123
Ob.
Hn.
S. Vc.
1
Vn.
2
Va.
Vc.
D.B.
128
129
Ob.
Hn.
S. Vc.
129
1
Vn.
2
Va.
Vc.
D.B.

46

42455

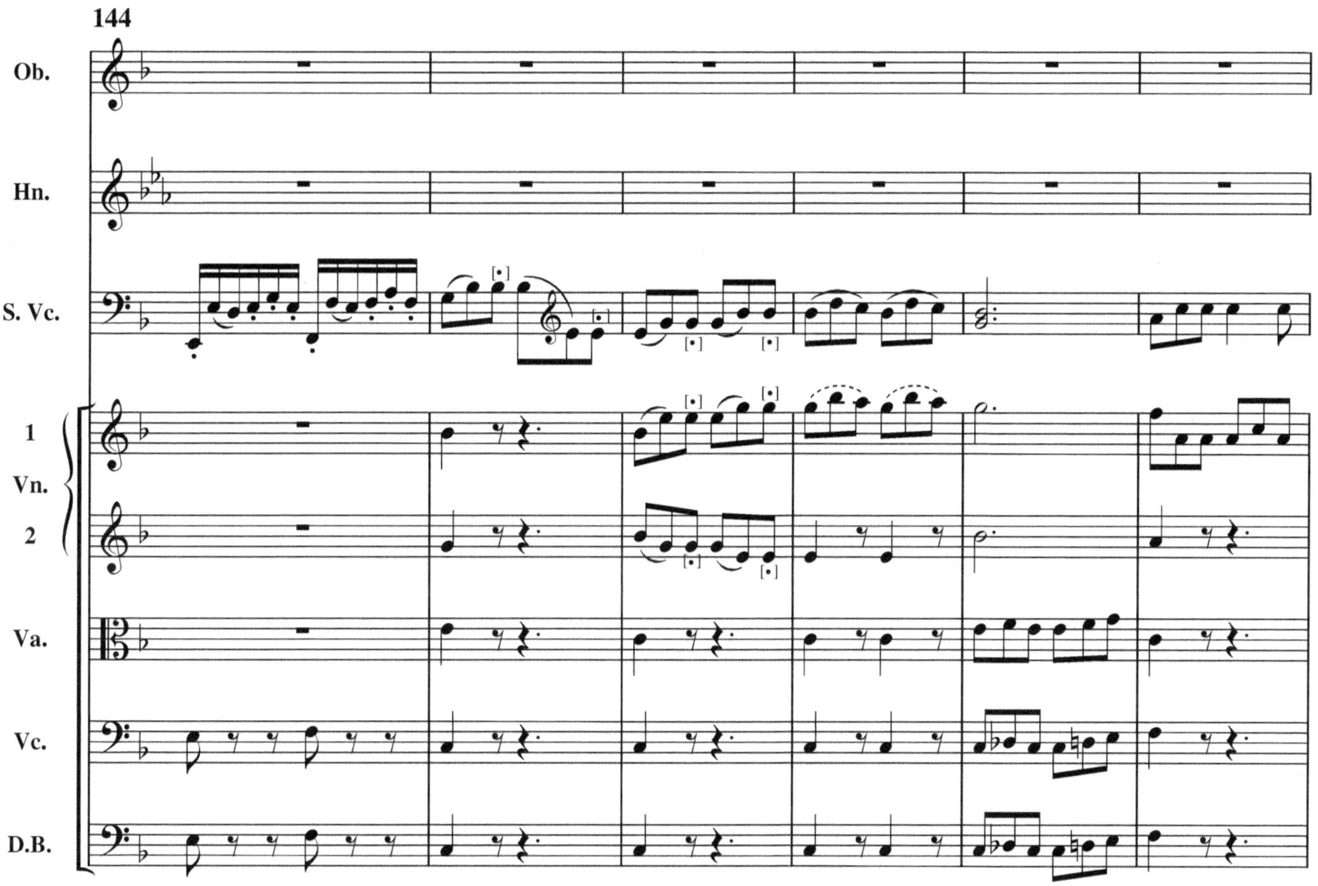
144
Ob.
Hn.
S. Vc.
1
Vn.
2
Va.
Vc.
D.B.

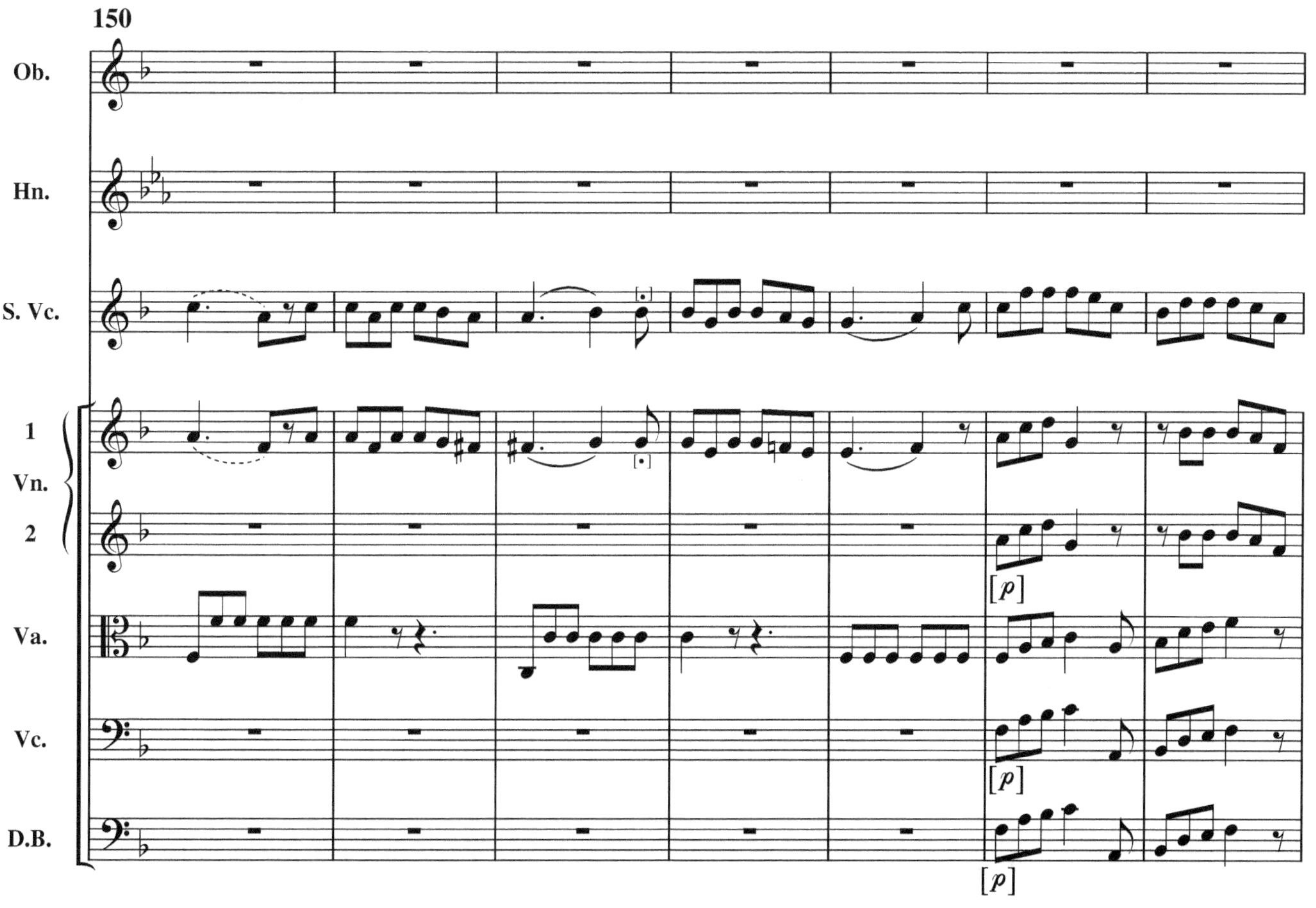
150
Ob.
Hn.
S. Vc.
1
Vn.
2
[p]
Va.
Vc.
[p]
D.B.
[p]

48

42455

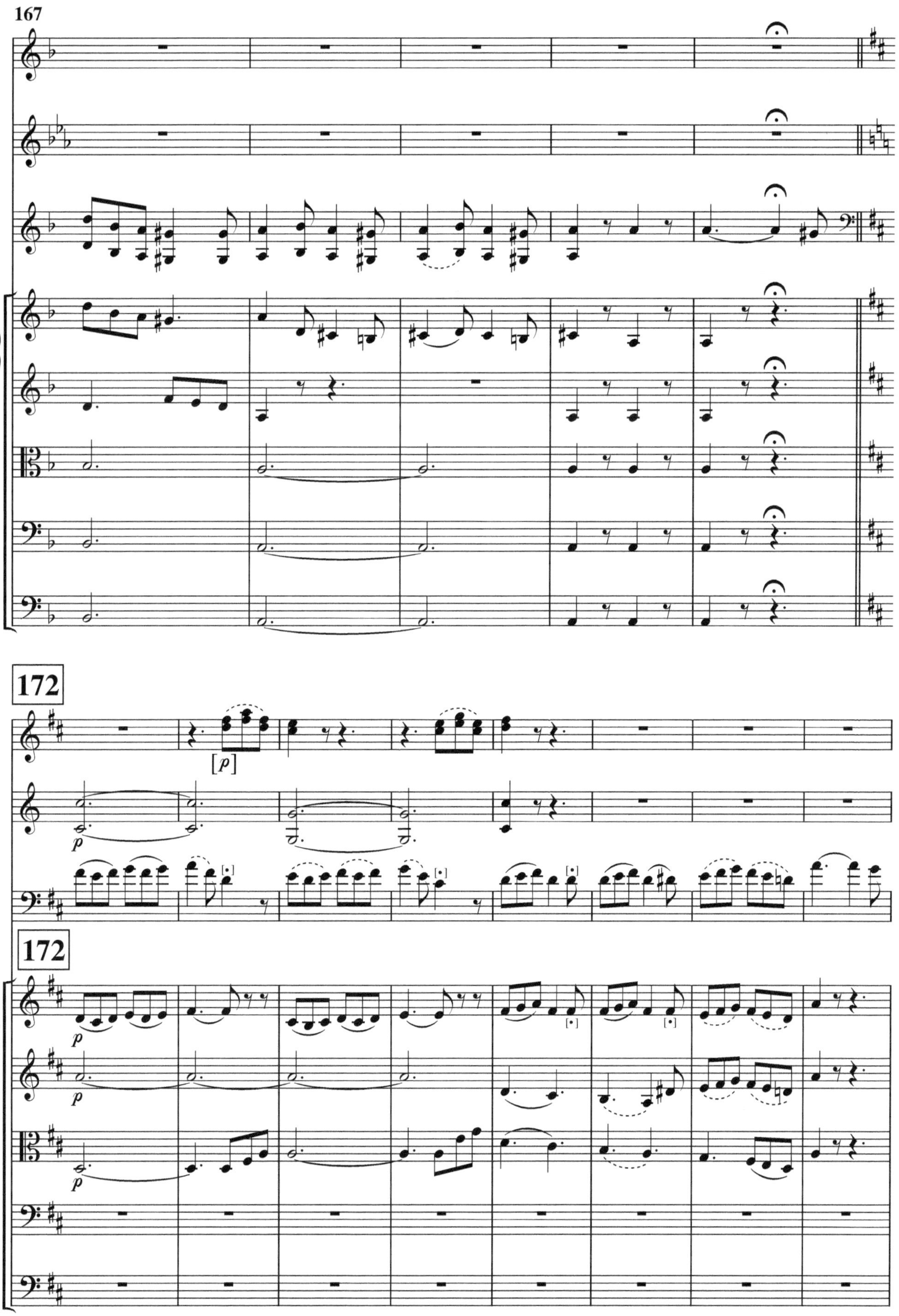
167
Ob.
Hn.
S. Vc.
1
Vn.
2
Va.
Vc.
D.B.
172
[p]
p
172
p
p
p

180
Ob.
Hn.
S. Vc.
180
1
Vn.
2
Va.
Vc.
D.B.
f
188
192
Ob.
Hn.
S. Vc.
192
1
Vn.
2
Va.
Vc.
D.B.
p

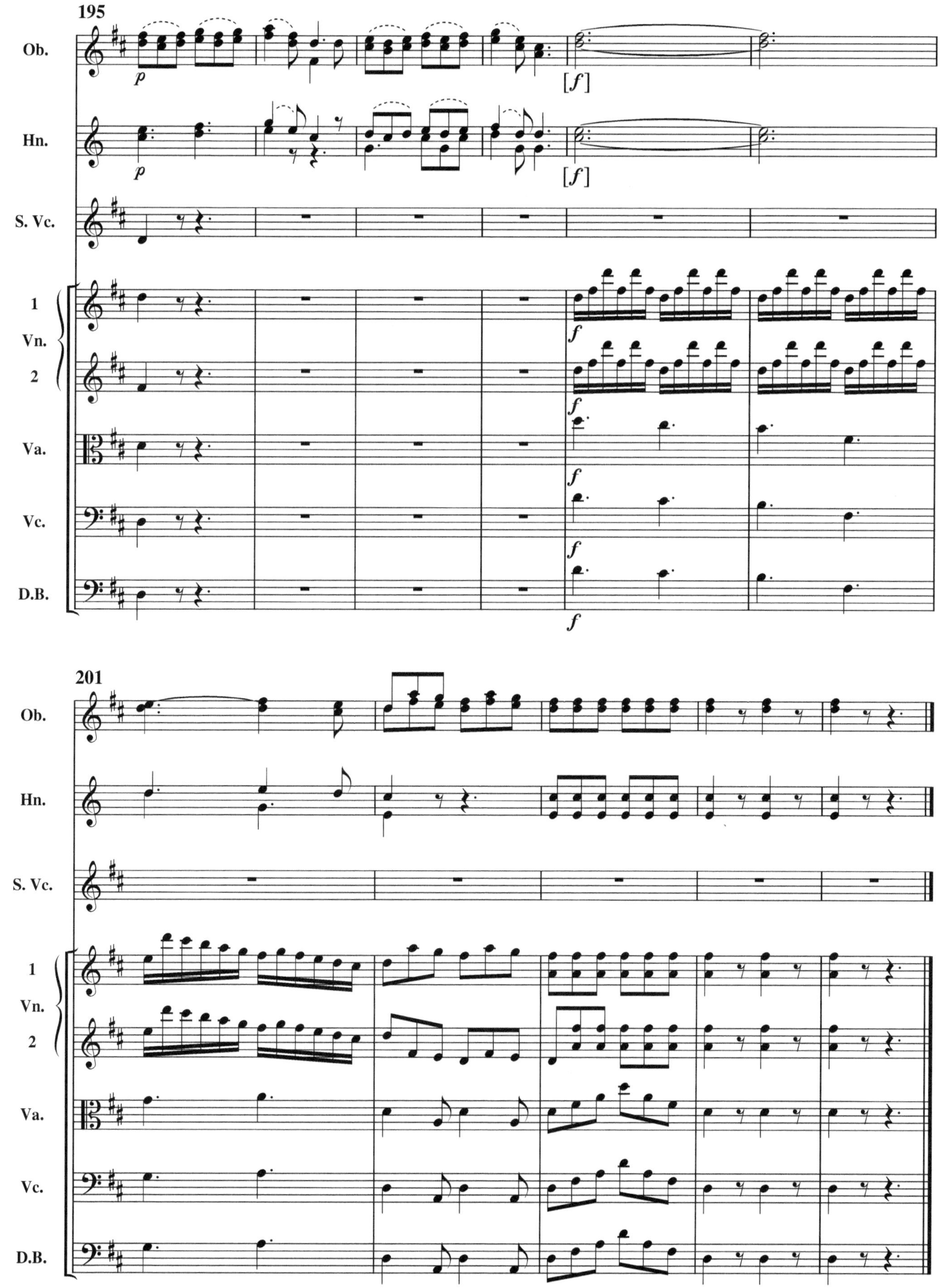
195
Ob.
Hn.
S. Vc.
1
Vn.
2
Va.
Vc.
D.B.
p
[f]
f
201